Eisenberg Originals

Eisenberg Originals
The Golden Years of Fashion, Jewelry, and Fragrance, 1920s-1950s
Sharon G. Schwartz and Laura Sutton
Schiffer Publishing Ltd
4880 Lower Valley Road • Atglen, PA 19310

To Ava and Max, with love from Grandma Sharon.
"I love you to the ends of the Earth."
–Sharon

Thanks to my family for… well, everything. With all my love.
–Laura

Other Schiffer Books on Related Subjects:
200 Years of American Manufactured Jewelry & Accessories, Suzanne Marshall, ISBN 978-0-7643-1838-2
All That Glitters, J. L. Lynnlee, ISBN 978-0-7643-0850-5
American Jewelry Manufacturers, Dorothy T. Rainwater, ISBN 978-0-88740-120-6

Library of Congress Control Number: 2016956296

Designed by Danielle D. Farmer
Cover design by John Cheek
Type set in Face of Yesterday/Caviar Dreams

Title Page:
Eisenberg & Sons catalog, copyright 1944. *Eisenberg Originals* illustration of 1944 fashion and jewelry for Joseph Spiess, Elgin, Illinois. (Unidentified illustrator) *Courtesy of D. Brett Benson, Inc. West Palm Beach, FL.*

Vase of Flowers Fur Clip. Marked Eisenberg Original and Sterling, mid-1940s. Gold vermeil. Three pieces form this detailed bouquet. Open-backed amethyst rhinestones of varying cuts form the vase and flowers. Gold leaves and clear pavé and bezel-set accents. 4¼" × 2½"

Amethyst Fur Clip. Marked Eisenberg Original and Sterling, mid-1940s. Gold wash. A huge faceted amethyst oval tops the piece with golden spikes dripping below, half of which are tipped with amethyst teardrops. 3" × 2½"

ISBN: 978-0-7643-5234-8
Printed in China

Published by Schiffer Publishing, Ltd.
4880 Lower Valley Road
Atglen, PA 19310
Phone: (610) 593-1777; Fax: (610) 593-2002
E-mail: Info@schifferbooks.com
Web: www.schifferbooks.com

For our complete selection of fine books on this and related subjects, please visit our website at www.schifferbooks.com. You may also write for a free catalog.

Schiffer Publishing's titles are available at special discounts for bulk purchases for sales promotions or premiums. Special editions, including personalized covers, corporate imprints, and excerpts, can be created in large quantities for special needs. For more information, contact the publisher.

We are always looking for people to write books on new and related subjects. If you have an idea for a book, please contact us at proposals@schifferbooks.com.

Contents

Acknowledgments

We have come across so many people who share our enthusiasm for Eisenberg. Whether through conversation, our purchase of wonderful additions to our collections, or their written contributions to an endless number of websites, we have developed relationships that have enhanced our desire to learn and ultimately to write this book.

Bobye Syverson, widely known as the "Queen of Eisenberg," began collecting Eisenberg jewelry and fashion before WWII. She has chronicled her vast collection, including rarely seen advertisements, scarves, and handbag accessories, in Jewel Chat, an online magazine at Jane Clarke's website, morninggloryjewelry.com. Syverson says, "I have always loved glitter…beads, sequins, rhinestones, diamonds. I spent my monthly allowance of $1 at the jewelry center in Woolworth's. That was during the Depression and $1 was a lot of money. I graduated from high school, went to college, and along came World War II. I got a job and discovered the wonders of layaway! I was interested only in the big Eisenberg pieces with the colorless stones. By the time I was seriously collecting, prices had gone up, and up. Now I buy only unusual pieces. My most expensive piece is a $3,000 pin. I have about 700 pieces."

Jane H. Clarke is an avid collector of both vintage costume and fine jewelry. She owns a store in Albuquerque, New Mexico, called Morning Glory Antiques and Jewelry, and hosts Jewel Chat, an online magazine at www.morninggloryjewelry.com. "When I heard that a book about Eisenberg jewelry was being written, I was thrilled," she says. "It is a book that we have needed for so long. The jewelry was carried by the best shops and stores. One vintage ad states that Eisenberg jewelry could be described as "Clusters of icy brilliance, shimmering like frozen fire!"

Teresa Knowles is a well-known collector who has owned some of the rarest examples of Eisenberg fashions, jewelry, and perfume. Over time, we have bought exceptionally rare pieces from her collection, and Teresa has become a friend and a wealth of knowledge. She says, "I cannot fully express how much pleasure I have gotten by collecting Eisenberg. I was first introduced to the Eisenberg line by browsing local antique stores. I began collecting right away and loved searching the flea markets, estate sales, and online markets to add new pieces to my growing collection. Even after all these years of collecting, I am surprised when I see designs I never knew existed. The imagination and talent that went into making these creations is delightful."

Carole and Stan Smith, owners of Ralph Singer Co. in Chicago, allowed us to use some of the recently discovered Eisenberg design cards from a time when their company was known as Agnini & Singer.

Steve Kravitz took the pictures of Sharon's collection. We appreciate the many hours he spent shooting and organizing the images. Steve is a native of Philadelphia and a graduate of Drexel University. The owner and co-founder of the commercial photography studio Unique Perspectives, he has worked on websites and print media and has done a great deal of work for fundraisers and team events.

Introduction

Eisenberg & Sons Inc. was one of the first American design houses. The jewelry that bears their mark is among the finest costume pieces ever created. Yet there is surprisingly little written about them, and almost nothing about the other products they marketed. In *Eisenberg Originals* we take the reader from their beginnings in fashion to the facts behind their revered jewelry line. Along the way we use pieces and ephemera to showcase the designs from the fashion and jewelry lines, but we also chronicle the fragrances, cosmetics, and accessories that are often overlooked. We outline the materials, signatures, and labels used through the years and reveal the people and the companies that were integral to their success during the golden years. Eisenberg Original creations deserved the place they held in only the finest of stores.

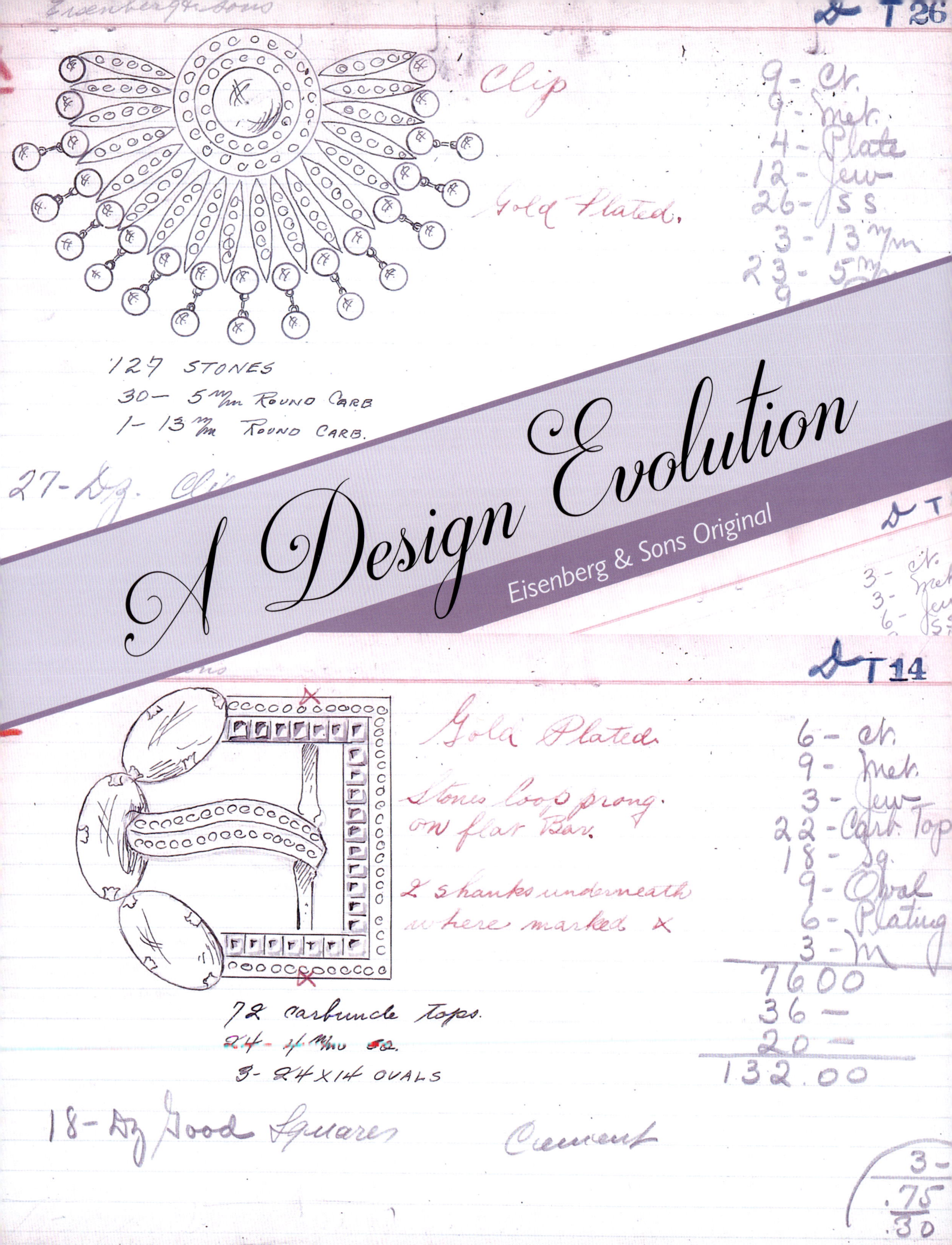
A Design Evolution
Eisenberg & Sons Original
Clip
Gold Plated.
127 STONES
30— 5 m/m ROUND CARB
1- 13 m/m ROUND CARB.
Gold Plated.
Stones loop prong on flat Bar.
2 shanks underneath where marked ×
72 carbuncle tops.
3- 24X14 OVALS
18-Dz Good Squares
Cement
132.00

An Eisenberg Company advertisement appearing in *Women's Wear Daily* on January 9, 1950, stated that Jonas Eisenberg created the company in 1914 and that it was the first label line in America. According to the obituary for Jonas Eisenberg in *Women's Wear Daily* on November 8, 1945, the story is actually a bit more complicated than that. Jonas immigrated to the United States in 1884; he married, started a family, and worked in the fashion industry for thirty years before founding a dress company with his brother, Julius, in 1914. However, this partnership would dissolve within five years, and Jonas would move his family to Chicago.

Jonas, now in his mid-fifties, formed a partnership with sons Harold and Sam, both in their twenties, and they re-launched the company around 1920. Eisenberg & Sons did not become Eisenberg & Sons Inc. until the company was incorporated in 1928, when Jonas stepped back from running the business and Harold became the president and Sam the secretary-treasurer. Jonas would remain as a board member until his passing at age eighty-one.

In the beginning, Eisenberg & Sons was solely a dress manufacturing company whose label, Eisenberg & Sons Original, was defined by luxurious designs that showcased impeccable taste. Every garment with an Eisenberg & Sons Original label had meticulous detailing and quality finishing that made it a fit for the exclusive dress shops the company was targeting.

There is little information from the company's very early days, possibly because it did not start advertising until later. However, on July 31, 1922, the *New York Tribune* ran an advertisement for the arrival of new Eisenberg & Sons fall cloth and silk dresses at S. J. Kasindorf, 38 West 32nd Street, Chicago. And an Eisenberg & Sons Original dress shown at the Spring Chicago Apparel Show was reviewed by *Women's Wear Daily* on February 1, 1927. The description reads, "Nile Green and Black Are Combined in a One-Piece Frock with Definitely Bloused Line. The Upper Part of the Bodice and Kimono Sleeve Are of Nile Green Canlon, while the Lower Section is of Black."

In reviews of Eisenberg fashions dating back to the twenties, the use of color and patterning is often mentioned, yet the Eisenberg Original label is most famous for little black dresses with couture touches. This image of conservative styling was created in part by white lace accents, which displayed magnificently against a black background. It was also this classic black-and-white look that Eisenberg would favor for most of its future advertising. Many of these creations were, in fact, available in a range of colors.

In a *Women's Wear Daily* letter published on July 25, 1929, Harold Eisenberg wrote that the company had been "skeptical about entering into advertising" and had resisted *Women's Wear Daily's* entreaties for three years before giving in. He wrote that they had advertised in three issues and that each ad had generated at least three accounts. They took marketing and advertising seriously from then on.

As the country plunged into the Great Depression, Eisenberg & Sons began to flourish. At a time when many companies were disappearing, it showed consistent growth. In 1929, it hosted three showings daily of designs for a variety of ages.

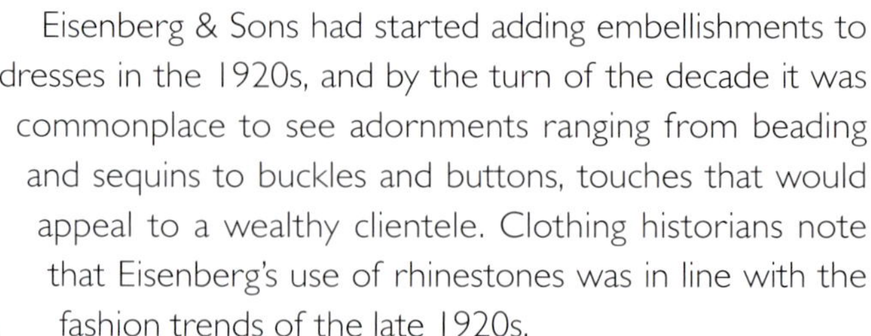

Eisenberg & Sons had started adding embellishments to dresses in the 1920s, and by the turn of the decade it was commonplace to see adornments ranging from beading and sequins to buckles and buttons, touches that would appeal to a wealthy clientele. Clothing historians note that Eisenberg's use of rhinestones was in line with the fashion trends of the late 1920s.

With a national ad campaign and expansion under way, the company increased its clothing enhancements for the Original label. While initially these sparkling accents were used solely for practical applications—buttons on a dress or a buckle on a jacket, soon they were being added purely as ornamentation. By the mid-1930s, the Eisenberg & Sons Original label was in demand across the country.

Eisenberg & Sons was exclusive in its marketing approach, making its pieces available in only one select store per city. In some instances this would be a department store, but in many towns it would be a smaller couture dress shop. The company took its pieces "on the road" to show in shops whose profiles matched Eisenberg's high-style dresses.

As Caroline Rennolds Milbank wrote in *New York Fashion—The Evolution of American Style,* "During the 1930s the company specialized in little black dresses in wool, silk, or synthetic silk and in dinner clothes, almost always ornamented with beautifully made costume jewelry, belt buckles, buttons, clips, or pins, and in embroidery simulating costume jewelry."

This style was developed with the aid of designer Irma Kirby, who was with the company at its inception in 1920. When it was incorporated in 1928, she was named vice president and given a share in the company. Some rare creations on the Original label bear her name, and the company advertised that she was one of America's most experienced and creative designers. The ads claimed that only an American designer such as Kirby could keep up with the rapidly changing tastes of American women and stated proudly that she understood the heart of American women and was never influenced by Europe.

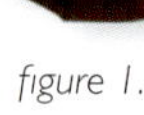

figure 1.1

figure 1.2

figure 1.3

An ad in *Vogue* on March 1, 1934, reads, "Originality, skill, and the finest of materials all combine to place her models in the leading style stores of the nation." In 1932, Gimbel Brothers of Philadelphia picked Kirby to be a principal designer in a fashion show honoring American-designed fashions. A fellow honoree was Lilly Daché, the most famous American milliner of her time.

Eisenberg & Sons' clothing was now beginning to attract widespread attention. By 1935, Carson Pirie Scott & Co. of Chicago showed the Originals line in its coveted North Room. Even the simplest day dresses had pleats, tucks, lace, or some form of accent to make it just a bit more eye-catching than the clothes of competitors. Each garment was crafted with such care and attention that every drape was perfect, no matter how many pieces it took to achieve the look. And with a reputation established, Eisenberg began making suits, coats, and matching ensembles.

figure 1.1 Burgundy Silk Velvet Dress. Labeled with the earliest Eisenberg & Sons Original label design, c. 1930s. Silk velvet evening dress in a rich burgundy hue. The material is surprisingly thin and lightweight.

figure 1.2 Bodice flowers add drama. Done in the same silk velvet, the many layers of petals are centered with pompoms.

figure 1.3 The sleeves end in dramatic poufs. Eisenberg's designer, Irma Kirby, loved to use sleeve detailing.

figure 1.4

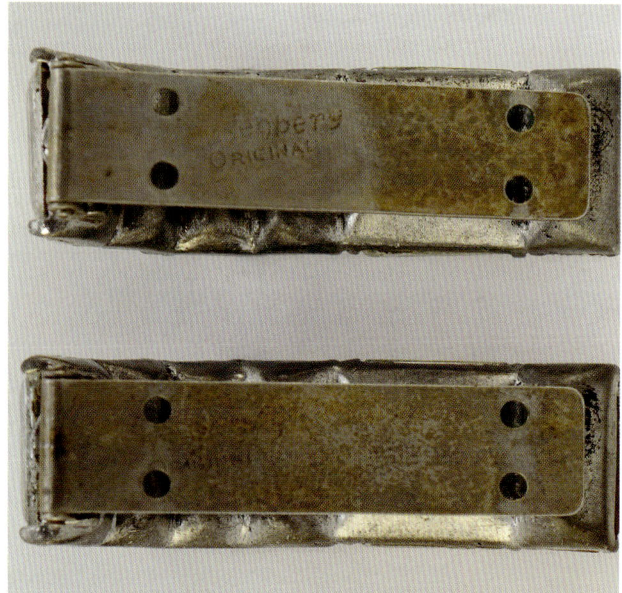

figure 1.5

figure 1.4 Pair of Baguette Sew-On Clips. Marked Eisenberg Original, c. 1940. These clips are hinged to hold fabric, but the back is designed to be sewn onto the garment. White pot metal with alternating rows of large, clear baguette rhinestones. 1½" × ⅝".

figure 1.5 Rear view showing the holes for attaching to the garment and the Eisenberg Original mark.

figure 1.6

figure 1.7

In addition to expanding the clothing lines in the 1930s, the Eisenbergs took their first steps into the world of jewelry. Rhinestone dress accents evolved as individual jewelry pieces that were sewn onto the dress to finish the look.

By the mid-1930s, Eisenberg & Sons was elaborately presenting these accents independent of the dresses. While the removable jewelry pieces were sold only with their specific garment, they came packaged in a blue velvet box. The adornments were an integral part of the vision of each dress, yet now the jewels could be removed or even worn with a different garment. Women raced to own these bold pieces, solidifying the company's place in fashion history as the first dress company to make jewelry that complemented its fashions. Eisenberg & Sons did not design this jewelry. The more elaborate decorations originated from a partnership with Agnini & Singer, a Chicago-based company.

figure 1.8

figure 1.6 Black Rayon Crepe Dress with Original Sew-ons. Labeled Eisenberg Originals, c. 1940s. A rare sample of a dress retaining its original embellishments. Black satin bow collar is accented with clear rhinestone sew-on clips. Black satin also bands the sleeve edges.

figure 1.7 Inset pleated black satin back panel.

figure 1.8 Close-up of bodice showcasing the sew-on pieces and the Eisenberg Originals label, which dates this piece to 1940. This shows that the adornments continued for the life of the line.

figure 1.9

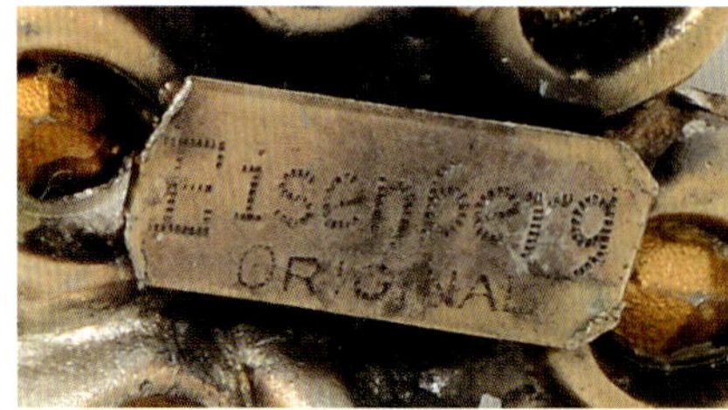

figure 1.10

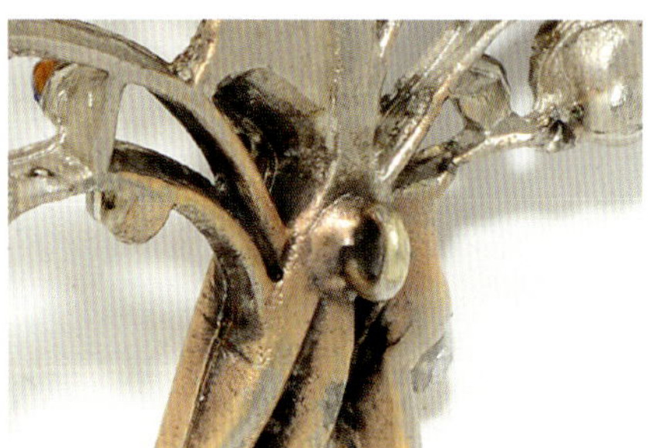

figure 1.10a

figure 1.9 Floral Sew-On. Marked Eisenberg Original, c. 1930s. Pot metal. Attached by rear loops. Clear rhinestone dimensional flower. Small blue rhinestone floral sprays arc off the clear-cut rhinestone stems. 2¾" × 1¼".

figure 1.10 & figure 1.10a Rear view showing the Eisenberg Original mark and the loops for attaching to the garment.

figure 1.11

figure 1.11 Rare Matched Pair of Adornments. Marked Eisenberg Original, c. 1930s. Two gold pot metal sew-ons with rear loops. Flowers made of emerald rhinestones with sprays of faux pearls bursting from the stems. 2¾" × 1¾".

figure 1.12 & figure 1.12a Rear view showing the Eisenberg Original mark and intricate design work. Rear loops at top and bottom for attaching.

figure 1.12

figure 1.12a

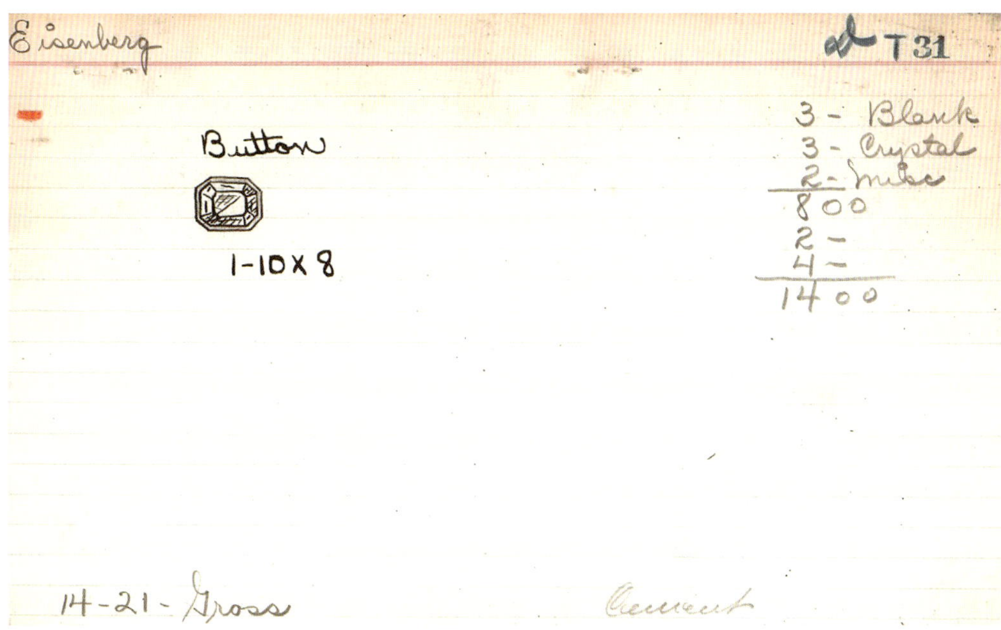

figure 1.13 Button design.

For a long time, no one was sure who produced these early accents. Then Susan Klein Bagdade, a jewelry author in Chicago, and Carole Smith, the owner of the Ralph Singer Company (formerly Agnini & Singer) searched the Agnini & Singer archives. There they discovered a treasure trove of design cards that chronicled pieces that Agnini & Singer had designed for various companies. Included were cards documenting art deco accent pieces for Eisenberg. These are amazing examples of how elaborate even the most basic item could become. The cards document the design, materials, and cost. One card shows an elaborate brooch, laying to rest the long-unanswered question of whether all of Eisenberg's jewelry was clips.

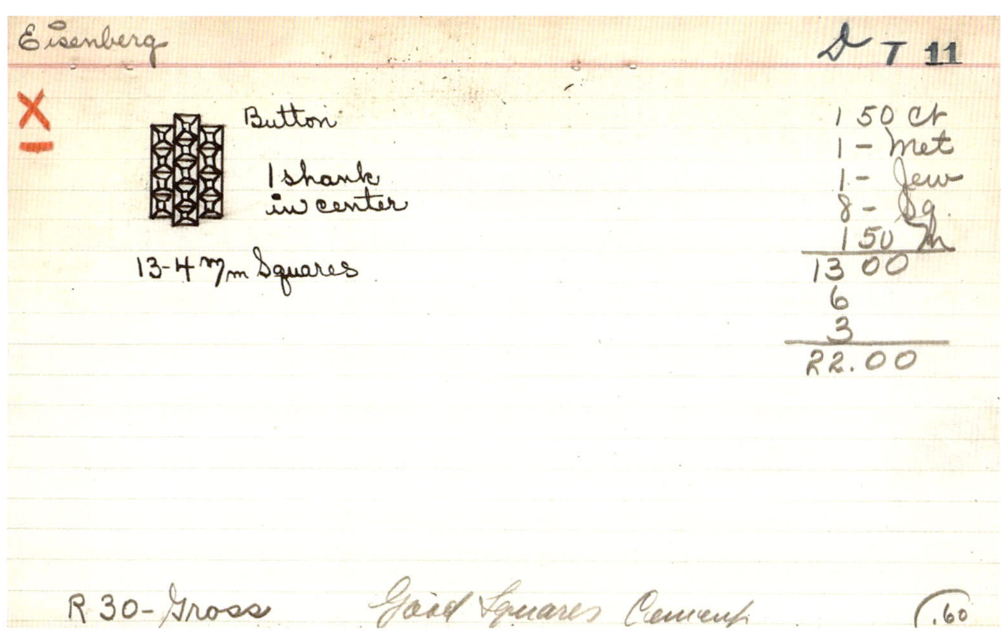

figure 1.14 Shank button design.

When the Eisenbergs later launched a full jewelry line, they severed their relationship with Agnini & Singer. Demand may have played a part in the decision, as Agnini & Singer may not have been able to handle the increased volume. Material concerns were also beginning to creep into the industry as the political situation in Europe declined, and contracting with companies in Rhode Island, the hub of the jewelry industry, may have seemed more secure. What is clear is that Agnini & Singer had set a precedent, and the look and quality of its jewelry continued in the new Eisenberg partnerships.

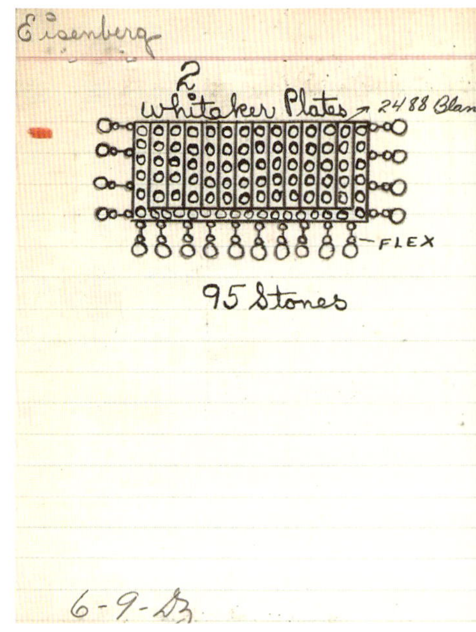

figure 1.15

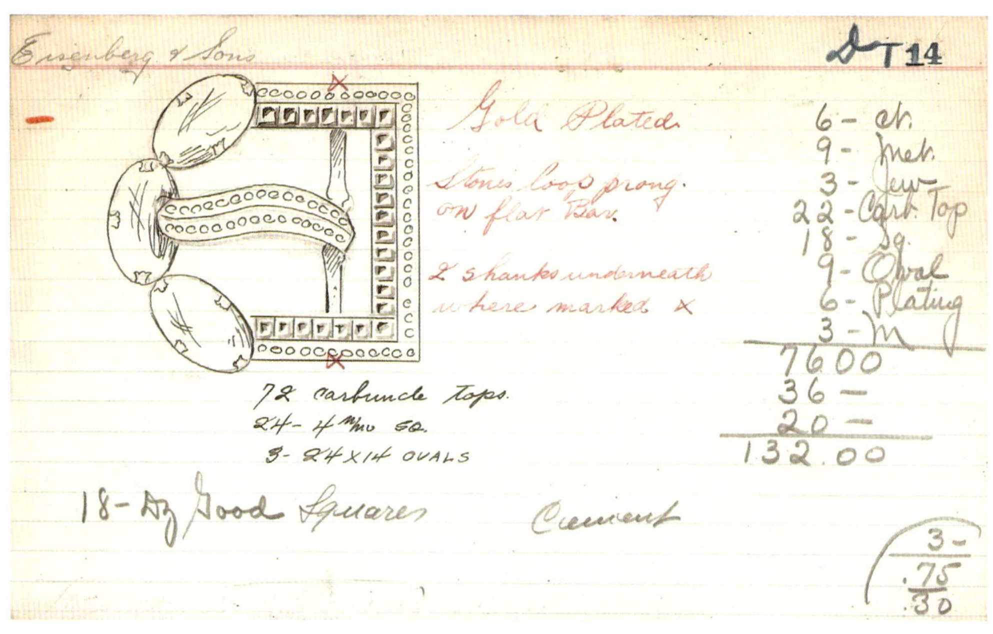

figure 1.17

figure 1.18

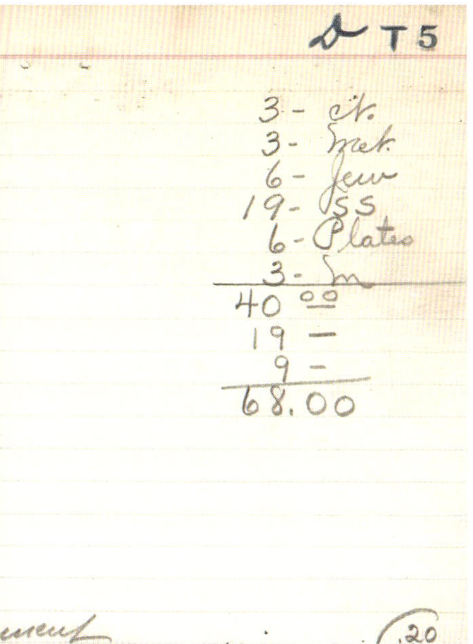

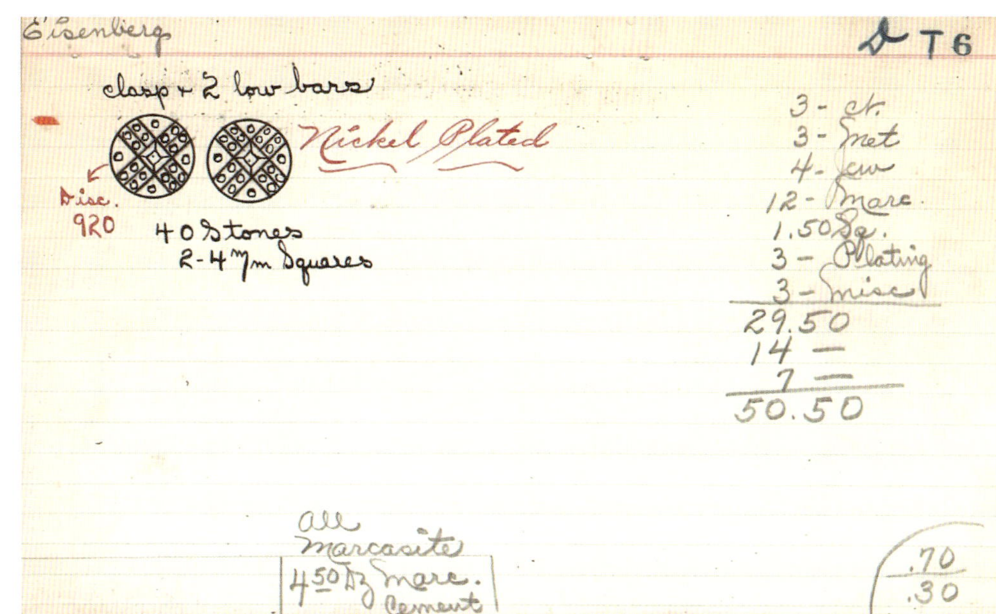

figure 1.16

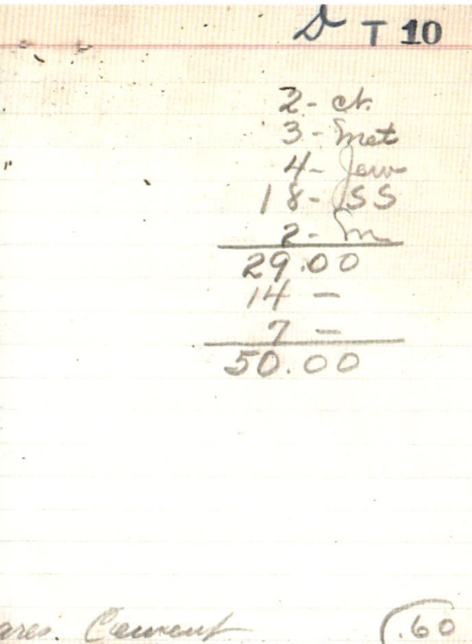

figure 1.19

figure 1.15 Unidentified design, includes ninety-five stones.

figure 1.16 Unidentified design, two discs.

figure 1.17 Ornate belt buckle.

figure 1.18 Possible belt buckle design.

figure 1.19 Clip, possibly leaf design, seventy-four stones.

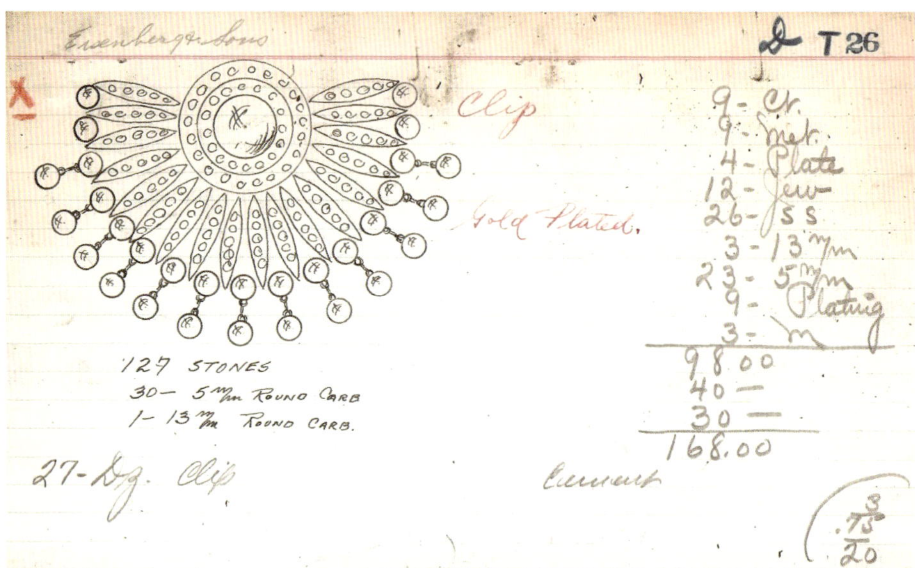

figure 1.20

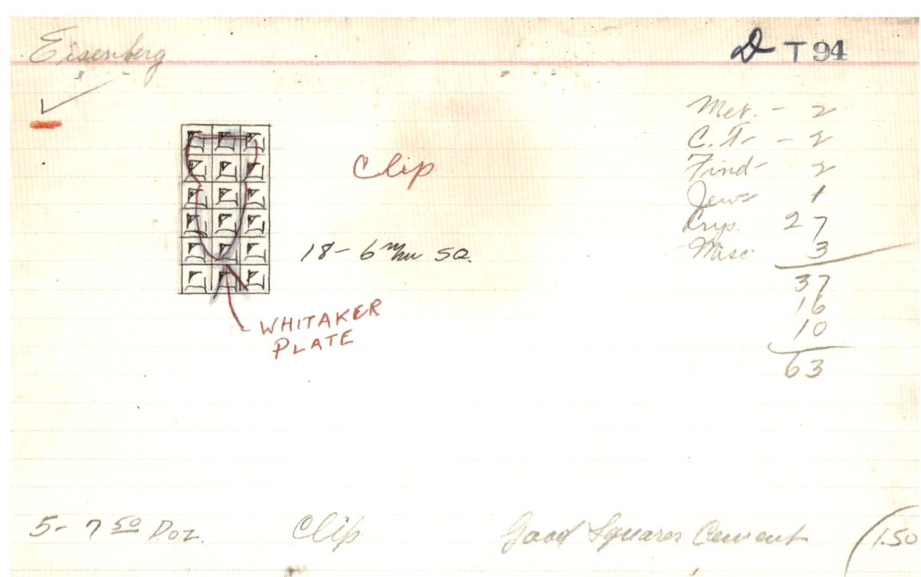

figure 1.21

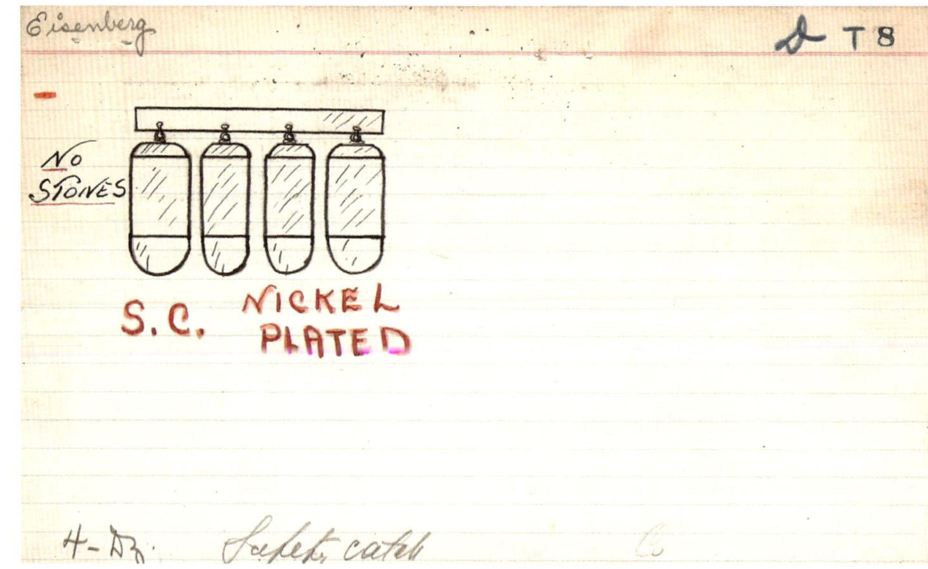

figure 1.22

figure 1.20 Clip with dangles, 127 stones.

figure 1.21 Note the hand-drawn outline of the dress clip.

figure 1.22 Not identified as a brooch; however, the design leaves little doubt that a pin is running along the top bar.

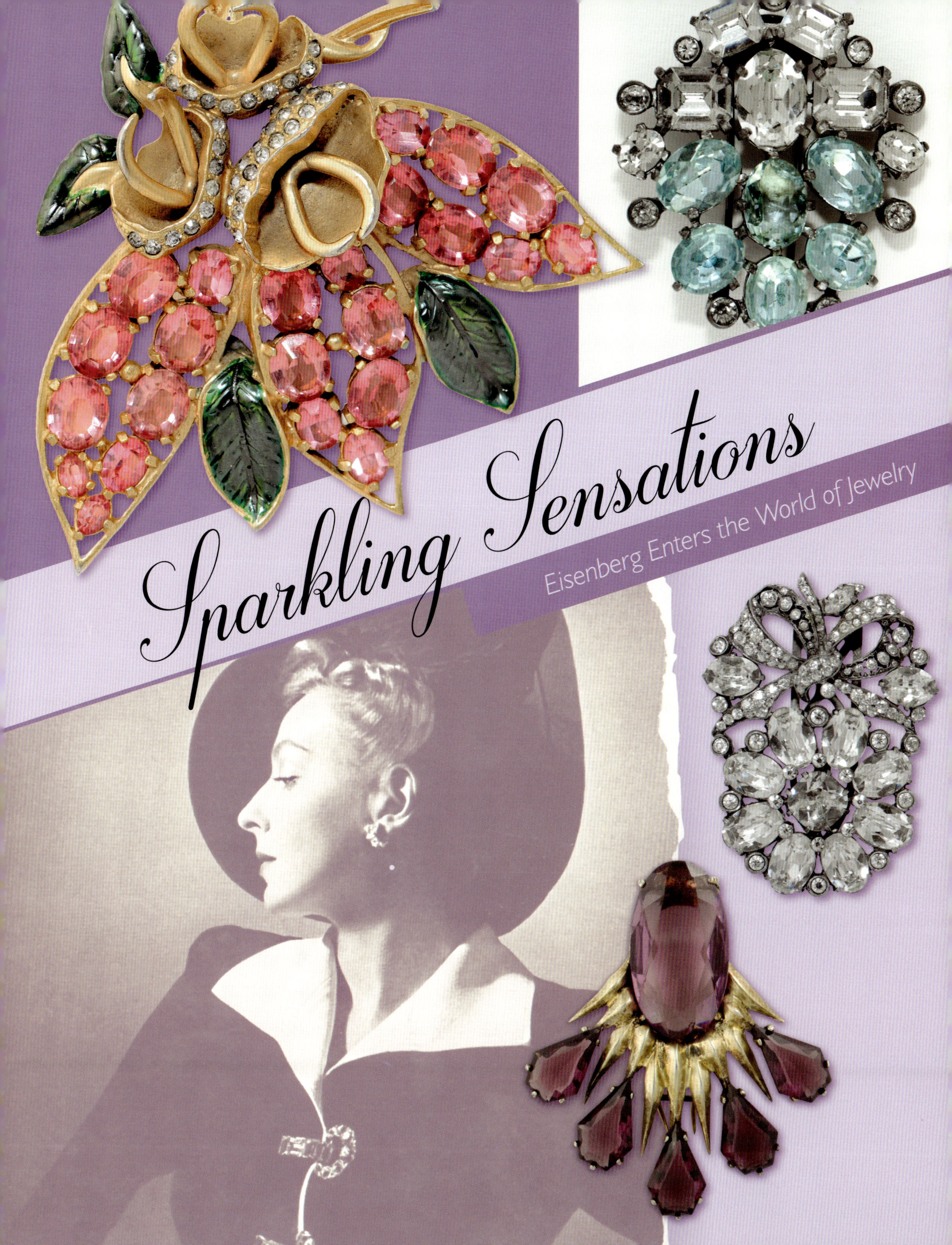

Sparkling Sensations

Eisenberg Enters the World of Jewelry

A myth persists regarding Eisenberg & Sons' expansion into jewelry. As the story goes, when the company began sewing jewelry on the clothing, and especially later when the pieces were merely clipped on, women were determined to have them, even if they didn't want the dress. The shoppers would take the garments into the dressing rooms, remove the jewels, and leave the dresses behind. This story is probably based on fact, but there was no theft epidemic so great that it triggered a jewelry line.

In a 2010 interview with *Collectors Weekly,* Sam Eisenberg's son, Karl, said that the chairman of Carson Pirie Scott & Co., one of Eisenberg & Sons' early small franchisees, told the family that they should pay attention to customers asking to buy only the jewelry.[1]

The increased interest in dresses with adornments, particularly removable clips, made Eisenberg & Sons realize that this suggestion made sense. Little did they know that the jewelry would be their legacy. In the interview with *Collector's Weekly*, Karl remembered that by the mid-1930s, the company had begun manufacturing a standalone jewelry line. It appeared in late 1930s advertising, and the first official product line traces to 1936, when Fallon & Kappel (F&K) became the company's main jewelry supplier. In the beginning, these pieces were made of pot metal and were mostly dress or fur clips.

Eisenberg's limited franchising meant that stores that wanted to sell the jewelry line also had to sell its other products. As Eisenberg expanded in the 1940s, this meant that stores carried a wide range of its products.

But creating a dedicated jewelry line was not without challenges, particularly finding a partner to handle the required volume. While F&K had been on the scene since 1936, production was still limited by the late 1930s, and few pieces had the styling that would come to define Eisenberg Original marked jewelry, according to *American Costume Jewelry—Art & Industry, 1935–1950* (Carla & Roberto Brunialti 2008).

It appears that Eisenberg spun the jewelry off into its own division—Eisenberg Jewelry, Inc.—at the end of 1940 or the beginning of 1941. By December 1941, the jewelry was established enough to be highlighted as an advertisers' choice for a holiday shopping spread in *Vogue*. The year 1941 would also see the first appearance of "Eisenberg Ice" in advertising, though it would not be trademarked until 1945.

In his 2010 interview with *Collectors Weekly*, Karl confirmed that his father, Sam, coined the phrase in reference to the gangster use of the word ice for diamonds, and it beautifully illustrated the diamond-like sparkle and amazing luster of the high-quality rhinestones and crystals. The crystals were primarily Austrian, and their sparkle came from their high lead content. Eisenberg particularly favored Swarovski rhinestones, known for their shine and unblemished purity.

Beginning in the late 1930s, Eisenberg contracted with a number of companies to design and manufacture its pot metal jewelry, including Agnini & Singer. Because Eisenberg's advertising was limited in the late 1930s, and Agnini & Singer did not mark its jewelry at that time, it is difficult to determine which pieces were designed exclusively for Eisenberg. Although Agnini & Singer's archival design cards, with "Eisenberg" written in the upper left corner, confirm that the manufacturer produced some of Eisenberg's exceptional pieces, Agnini & Singer apparently offered other clients many of the same designs.

While Eisenberg lists F&K as the jewelry supplier after 1936, at least one other vendor—Reinad Novelty Co.—is credited with contributing pot metal pieces, including figural designs. In addition, F&K was creating designs contributed by multiple freelancers even after 1940, when Ruth Kamke became their sole in-house designer. This means that pieces were coming from a variety of creative minds, allowing for a wide spectrum of styles even in one season.

The Eisenberg sons would travel to the F&K showroom and select pieces they thought would go well with their dress collections. These pieces did not bear the Eisenberg mark, either. Other companies bought similar pieces from F&K with their own company mark. Hence, duplicate designs appeared on the market.

Warman's Costume Jewelry Figurals—Identification and Price Guide (Flood 2007) references two Eisenberg Original creations that later appear under other company names, and that have also appeared unmarked. Flood believes that Reinad resold its designs for Eisenberg to other customers after Eisenberg discontinued the relationship.

Another source questioned whether Reinad was actually manufacturing exclusive pieces for it clients or was copying pieces from other companies.[2]

However the jewely came into being, the duplication of designs under different labels occurred in all the production houses. For example, Carla Brunialti and Roberto Brunialti noted that one Eisenberg Original piece was nearly identical to one with the Chanel mark. Another famous piece depicting an Asian man with gold vermeil was seen in a couple of variations marked Eisenberg Original. An identical piece was marked for Hattie Carnegie and also produced in unmarked variations.

What this highlights is that high-level costume jewelry was a small world. While many companies offered full production from design to delivery, apparently not many produced the grade that Eisenberg wanted.

Despite all this confusion, Eisenberg was, in fact, one of the first companies to mark their jewelry. While today it seems unthinkable to try to establish a brand without actually branding your products, it was not until the 1940s that it became common to do so in the industry. This means that there are thousands of high-quality unmarked pieces that will always remain "orphans."

Oddly, there are also a number of pot metal pieces marked Eisenberg Original that have glued-in stones, which was unusual for high-end manufacturers. Why would Eisenberg have contracted for lower quality "paste" pieces when hand-set, prong-mounted settings were part of the excellence Eisenberg was establishing?

Kamke was asked this question in an interview she gave in 2000, but she, too, was baffled.[3] Are these period counterfeits? Eisenberg placed an ad in *Women's Wear Daily* on June 6, 1941, urging customers to look for the Eisenberg Original mark to guarantee they were buying a real thing. Obviously, they were attempting to prevent knock-offs being presented as unmarked Eisenberg pieces.

By 1943 Eisenberg was one of F&K's core clients, and the jewelry line was still growing. With supplies becoming strained due to the war, hard choices needed to be made. Pot metal, the base for F&K's jewelry, was restricted to war manufacturing, and high-quality imported stones were becoming less available. It would have been a bad time for F&K to be buying more costly components without sales guarantees, and for Eisenberg to be competing for sales. So whether F&K won Eisenberg's loyalty, or the other way around, the two companies signed an exclusivity deal in 1943 that lasted for decades. (The exact date is not documented, but anecdotal sources agree on the year.)

On January 10, 1942, Florence Nathan, who worked for F&K, filed the only jewelry designs ever patented to Eisenberg. In the years to come, hardware designs were attributed to Eisenberg, but no other jewelry. Nathan did not design these pieces, but they bear her name because she filed the paperwork.

May 19, 1942. F. NATHAN Des. 132,445

PIN OR SIMILAR ARTICLE

Filed Feb. 14, 1942

INVENTOR.
Florence Nathan,
BY
Cromwell, Greist + Warden
attys.

figure 2.1 Patented fur clip. Marked Eisenberg Original, c. 1942. Silver pot metal with white crystals and rhinestones and square, round, and baguette stones. 2" × 2".

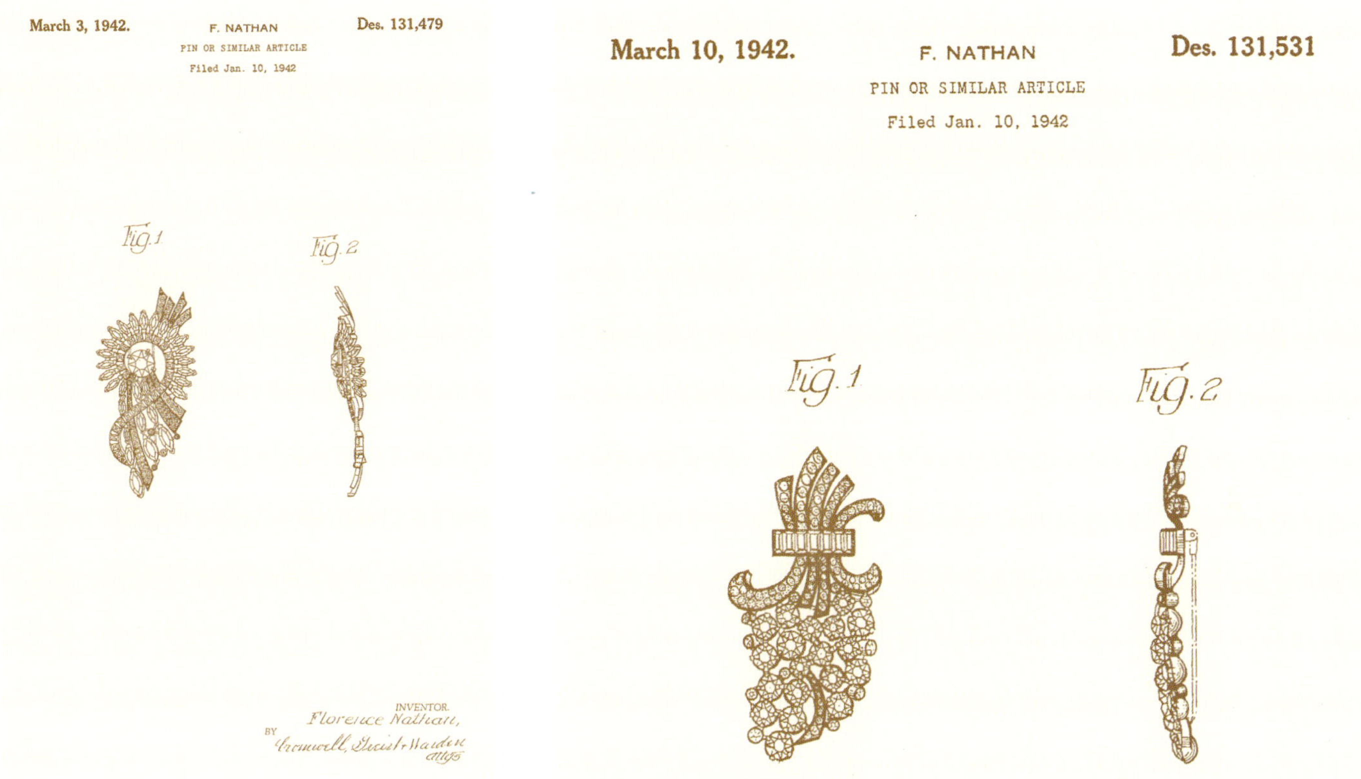

figure 2.2 Patented fur clip. Marked Eisenberg Original, c. 1942. Silver pot metal. Floral design with large prong-set stones accented by smaller pavé-set stones with a band of baguettes. Also marked with stone setter's mark number 22. 4" × 2⅛".

March 10, 1942. F. NATHAN Des. 131,530

PIN OR SIMILAR ARTICLE

Filed Jan. 10, 1942

Fig. 1 Fig. 2

INVENTOR.
Florence Nathan,
BY
Cromwell, Greist & Warden
attys.

March 24, 1942. F. NATHAN Des. 131,688

PIN OR SIMILAR ARTICLE

Filed Jan. 12, 1942

Fig. 1 Fig. 2

INVENTOR.
Florence Nathan,
BY
Cromwell, Greist & Warden,
attys.

May 19, 1942. F. NATHAN Des. 132,434

PIN OR SIMILAR ARTICLE

Filed Feb. 14, 1942

Fig. 1 Fig. 2

INVENTOR.
Florence Nathan,
BY
Cromwell, Greist & Warden
attys.

May 19, 1942. F. NATHAN Des. 132,436

PIN OR SIMILAR ARTICLE

Filed Feb. 14, 1942

Fig. 1 Fig. 2

INVENTOR.
Florence Nathan,
BY
Cromwell, Greist & Warden
attys.

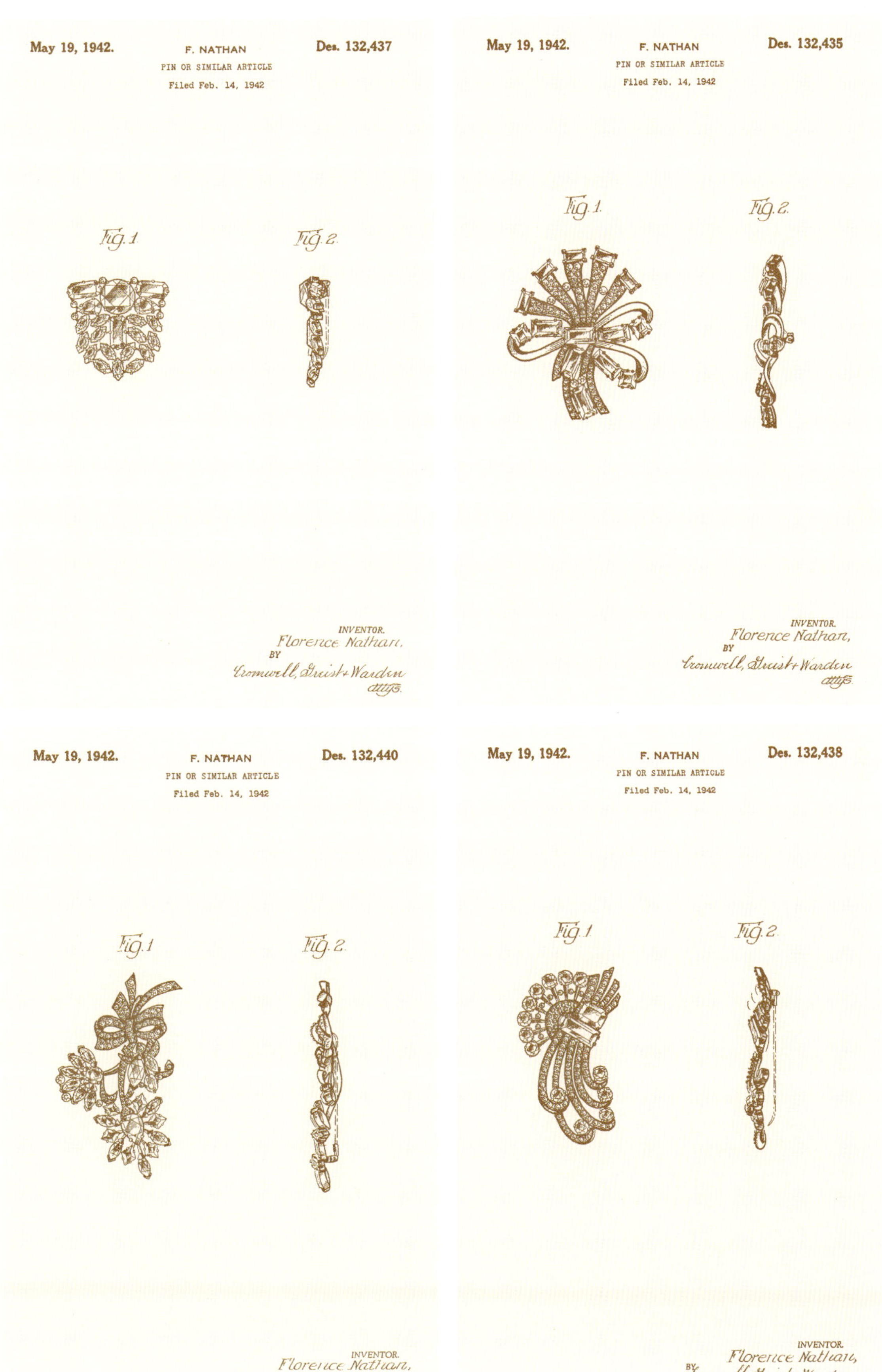
May 19, 1942. F. NATHAN Des. 132,437
PIN OR SIMILAR ARTICLE
Filed Feb. 14, 1942

Fig. 1 Fig. 2

INVENTOR.
Florence Nathan,
BY
Cromwell, Greist + Warden
attys.

May 19, 1942. F. NATHAN Des. 132,435
PIN OR SIMILAR ARTICLE
Filed Feb. 14, 1942

Fig. 1. Fig. 2.

INVENTOR.
Florence Nathan,
BY
Cromwell, Greist + Warden
attys.

May 19, 1942. F. NATHAN Des. 132,440
PIN OR SIMILAR ARTICLE
Filed Feb. 14, 1942

Fig. 1 Fig. 2.

INVENTOR.
Florence Nathan,
BY
Cromwell, Greist + Warden
attys.

May 19, 1942. F. NATHAN Des. 132,438
PIN OR SIMILAR ARTICLE
Filed Feb. 14, 1942

Fig. 1 Fig. 2.

INVENTOR.
Florence Nathan,
BY
Cromwell, Greist + Warden
attys.

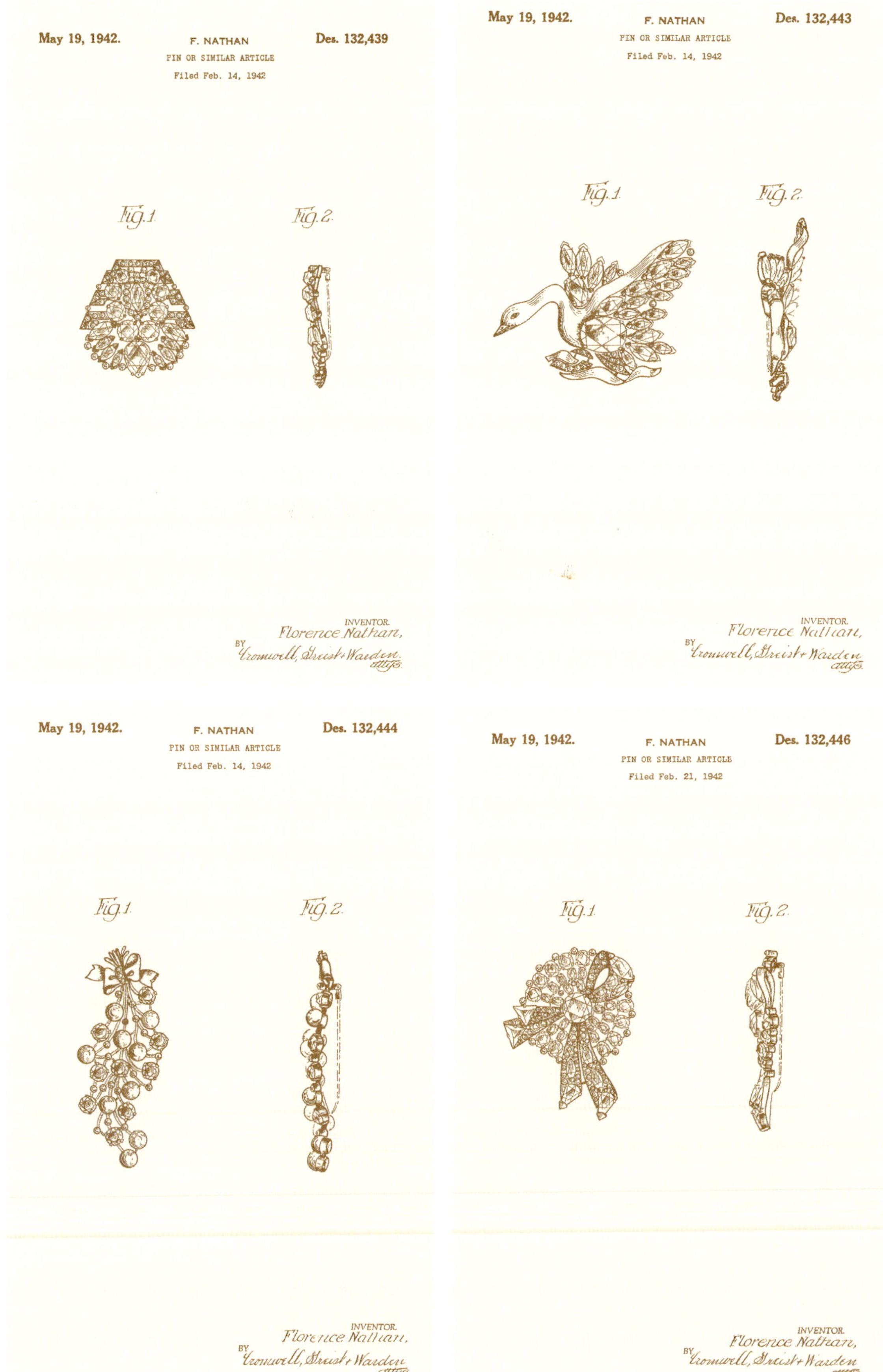
May 19, 1942. F. NATHAN Des. 132,439
PIN OR SIMILAR ARTICLE
Filed Feb. 14, 1942

May 19, 1942. F. NATHAN Des. 132,443
PIN OR SIMILAR ARTICLE
Filed Feb. 14, 1942

May 19, 1942. F. NATHAN Des. 132,444
PIN OR SIMILAR ARTICLE
Filed Feb. 14, 1942

May 19, 1942. F. NATHAN Des. 132,446
PIN OR SIMILAR ARTICLE
Filed Feb. 21, 1942

May 19, 1942. F. NATHAN Des. 132,449

PIN OR SIMILAR ARTICLE

Filed Feb. 21, 1942

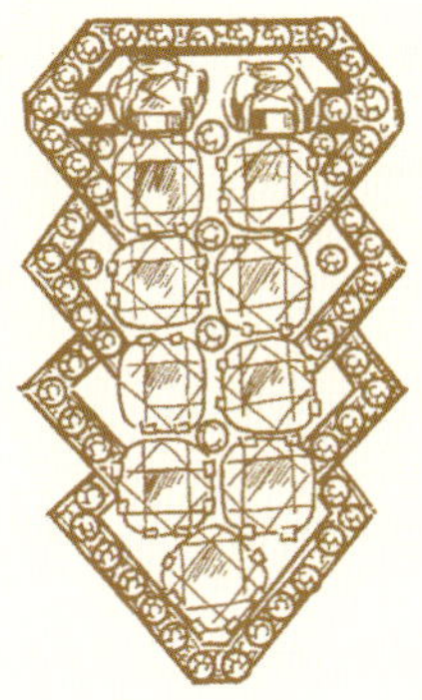

Fig. 2.

INVENTOR.
Florence Nathan,
BY
Cromwell, Greist & Warden
attys.

figure 2.3 Patented Fur Clip. Marked Eisenberg Original, c. 1942. Silver pot metal. Deco design of two rows of large clear rounds running down the center with standoff zigzag outline holding clear pavé set stones. Bezel set clear accents are spread throughout. 3¼" × 1¾".

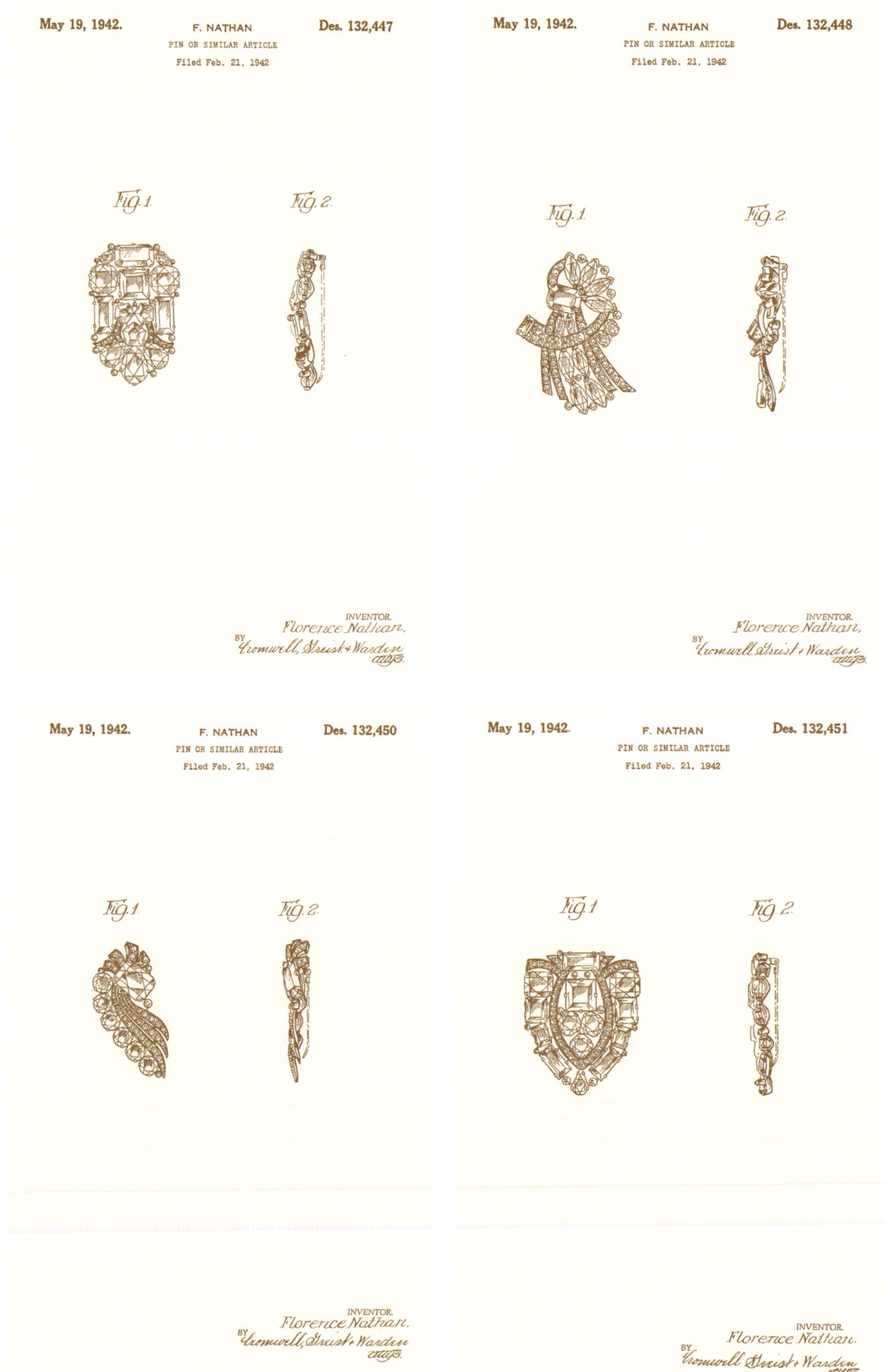
May 19, 1942.
F. NATHAN
Des. 132,447
PIN OR SIMILAR ARTICLE
Filed Feb. 21, 1942
Fig. 1
Fig. 2
INVENTOR.
Florence Nathan,
BY
Cromwell, Greist & Warden
attys.
May 19, 1942.
F. NATHAN
Des. 132,448
PIN OR SIMILAR ARTICLE
Filed Feb. 21, 1942
Fig. 1
Fig. 2
INVENTOR.
Florence Nathan,
BY
Cromwell, Greist & Warden
attys.
May 19, 1942.
F. NATHAN
Des. 132,450
PIN OR SIMILAR ARTICLE
Filed Feb. 21, 1942
Fig. 1
Fig. 2
INVENTOR.
Florence Nathan,
BY
Cromwell, Greist & Warden
attys.
May 19, 1942.
F. NATHAN
Des. 132,451
PIN OR SIMILAR ARTICLE
Filed Feb. 21, 1942
Fig. 1
Fig. 2
INVENTOR.
Florence Nathan.
BY
Cromwell, Greist & Warden
attys.

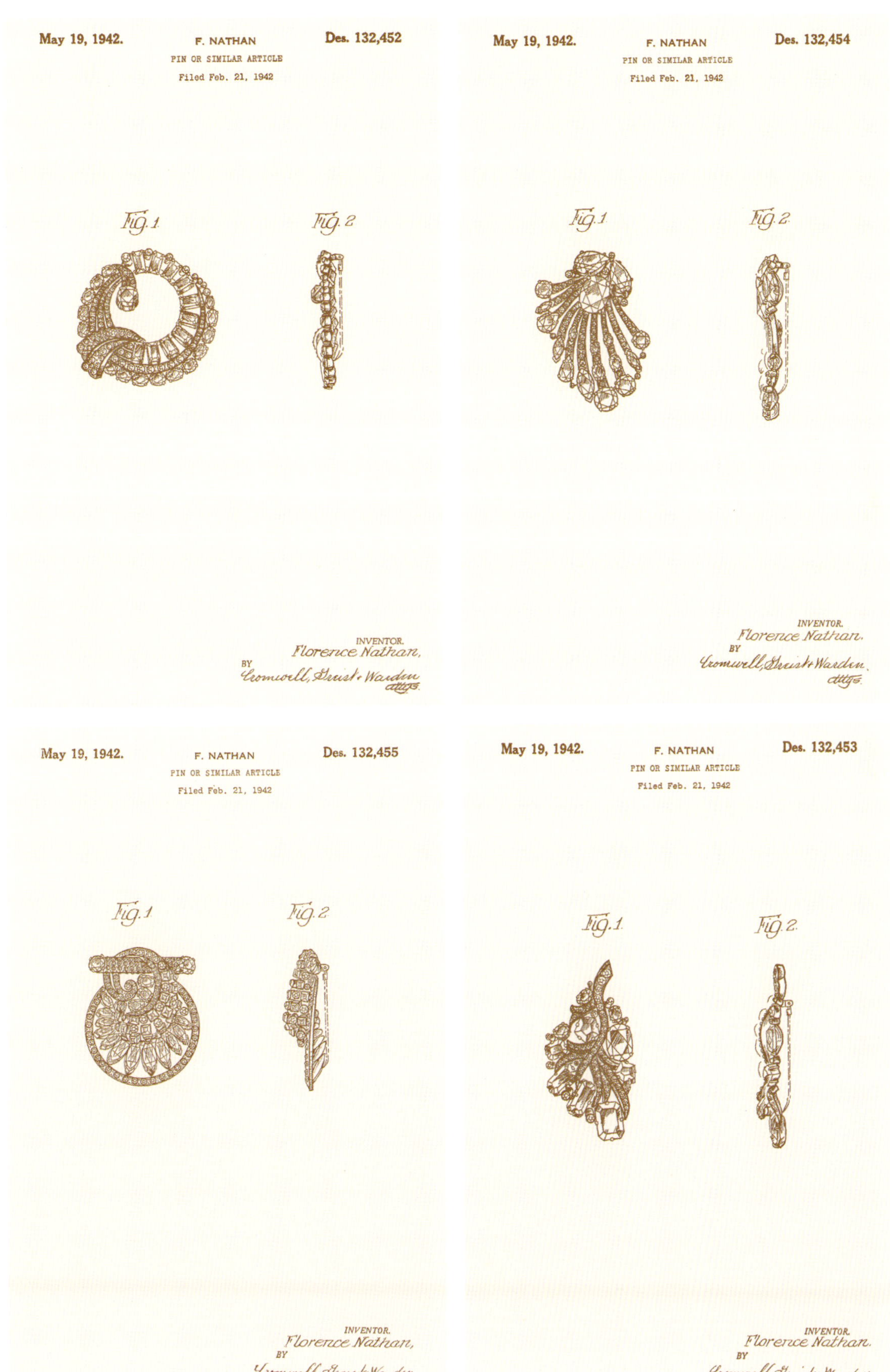
May 19, 1942.
F. NATHAN
Des. 132,452
PIN OR SIMILAR ARTICLE
Filed Feb. 21, 1942
Fig. 1
Fig. 2
INVENTOR.
Florence Nathan,
BY
Cromwell, Greist & Warden
attys.
May 19, 1942.
F. NATHAN
Des. 132,454
PIN OR SIMILAR ARTICLE
Filed Feb. 21, 1942
Fig. 1
Fig. 2
INVENTOR.
Florence Nathan.
BY
Cromwell, Greist & Warden.
attys.
May 19, 1942.
F. NATHAN
Des. 132,455
PIN OR SIMILAR ARTICLE
Filed Feb. 21, 1942
Fig. 1
Fig. 2
INVENTOR.
Florence Nathan,
BY
Cromwell, Greist & Warden
attys.
May 19, 1942.
F. NATHAN
Des. 132,453
PIN OR SIMILAR ARTICLE
Filed Feb. 21, 1942
Fig. 1
Fig. 2
INVENTOR.
Florence Nathan.
BY
Cromwell, Greist & Warden
attys.

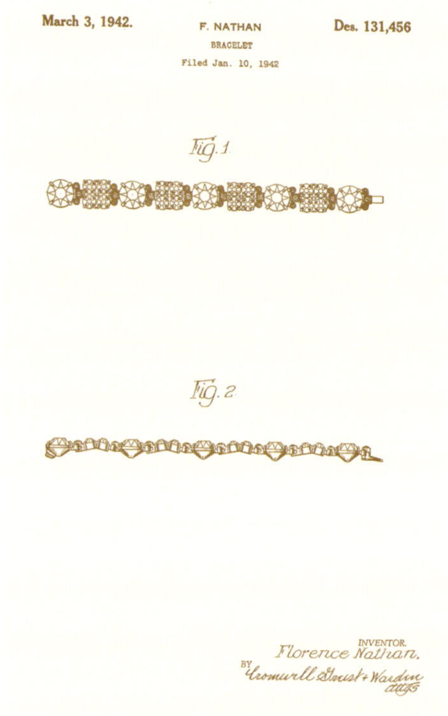

March 3, 1942. F. NATHAN Des. 131,456

BRACELET

Filed Jan. 10, 1942

Fig. 1

Fig. 2

INVENTOR.
Florence Nathan,
BY
Cromwell, Greist & Warden
attys.

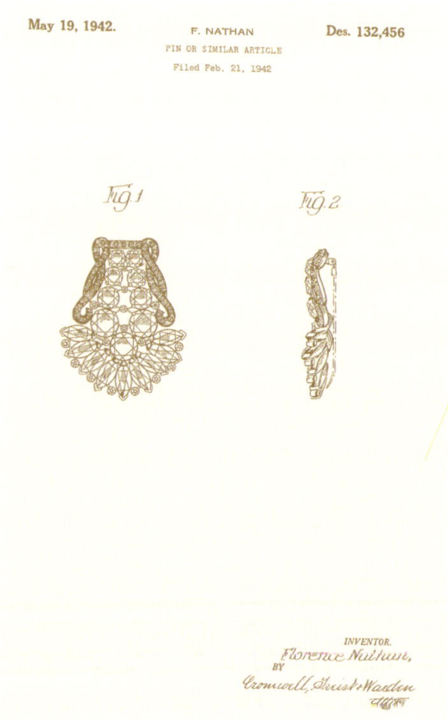

May 19, 1942. F. NATHAN Des. 132,456

PIN OR SIMILAR ARTICLE

Filed Feb. 21, 1942

Fig. 1 Fig. 2

INVENTOR.
Florence Nathan,
BY
Cromwell, Greist & Warden
attys.

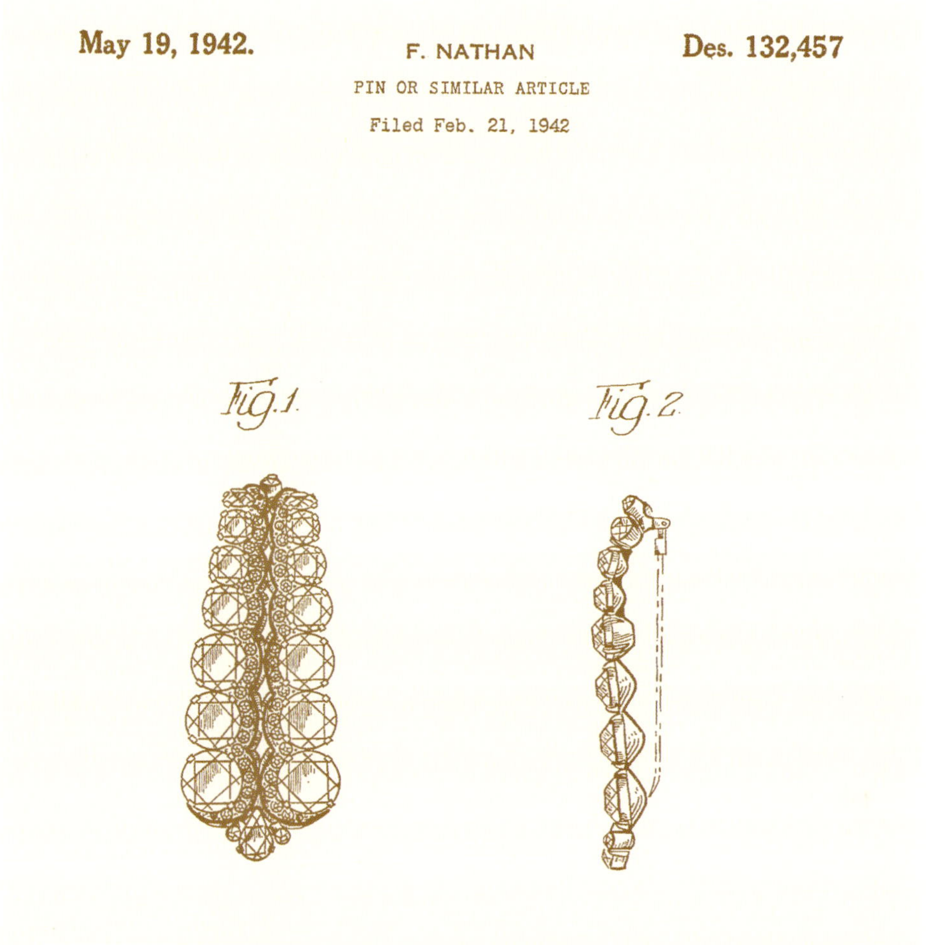

May 19, 1942. F. NATHAN Des. 132,457

PIN OR SIMILAR ARTICLE

Filed Feb. 21, 1942

Fig. 1. Fig. 2.

INVENTOR.
Florence Nathan,
BY
Cromwell, Greist & Warden
attys.

The availability of pot metal, used since the 1920s, was coming to an end as WWII approached. These basic metals were deemed necessary for military purposes, and in 1943 sterling replaced pot metal. The relationship with F&K sparked production of many different styles and colorful designs. Eisenberg proved its love for the "bow" with abstract and literal bows and styling elements that evoked ribbon loops and ties.

figure 2.4

figure 2.5

figure 2.6

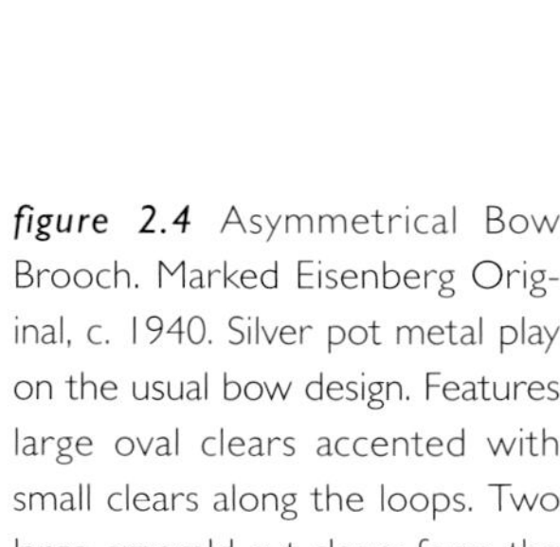

figure 2.4 Asymmetrical Bow Brooch. Marked Eisenberg Original, c. 1940. Silver pot metal play on the usual bow design. Features large oval clears accented with small clears along the loops. Two large emerald-cut clears form the center knot. 1¾" × 3".

figure 2.5 Large Stone Bow Brooch. Marked Eisenberg Original, c. 1940. Silver pot metal. The classic bow shape is done in clear oval stones graduated in size but all substantial. Edged and outlined with clear pavé set rounds. 2" × 3¾".

figure 2.6 Floral with Bow Dress Clip. Marked Eisenberg Original, c. 1940. Silver pot metal. Found in original box. Large clear ovals define the flower with bezel set clears as accents. Ribbon bow is done in clear pavé set rhinestones. 3" × 2½". Eisenberg Ice is a phrase that has been in use one way or another since Eisenberg took its first steps into jewelry. Characterized by their brilliant, clear sparkle, these are the icons of Eisenberg jewelry.

figure 2.7

figure 2.8

figure 2.9

figure 2.10

figure 2.7 Aqua and Clear Rhinestone Bow. Marked Eisenberg Original, c. 1940. The piece is set with massive aqua stones in cuts of emerald, oval, marquis, and teardrop. Clear rhinestones cover the rest of the solid pieces in this unique open space design. 2¼" × 3⅜".

figure 2.8 Turquoise and Faux Coral Bow Brooch. Marked Eisenberg Original, c. 1930s. Gold wash pot metal. Huge aqua stones of various cuts and sizes decorate the ribbon sections. With accent lines of clear pavé set rhinestones and scattered faux coral beads. 2" × 3".

figure 2.9 Bow Brooch. Marked Eisenberg Original and Sterling, mid-1940s. Bow is anchored by a large round clear with the ribbon loops holding large multi-cut prong set clears. Bezel set clears of various sizes add accent and small pavé set clears outline each section. 3" × 2¼".

figure 2.10 Unique Bow Brooch. Marked Eisenberg Original and Sterling, mid-1940s. Two massive, heavily faceted clear stones dominate this stunning piece. Much of the ribbon work is decorated with clear pavé sets. Bezel set clears form a unique little fan across the top. 2" × 3".

figure 2.11

figure 2.12

figure 2.13

figure 2.11 Intricate Bow Brooch. Marked Eisenberg Original & Sterling, mid-1940s. Bow is strands of clear pavé set stones running in layered rows, giving dimension. The open ribbon work is accented with clear marquis stones and finished with a large oval center stone. 2 ⅝" × 2¾".

figure 2.12 Abstract Fur Clip. Marked Eisenberg Original, c. 1940. Rare open design. Silver pot metal. Multiple shapes, cuts, and sizes of large, clear rhinestones with bezel-set clear accents and framing done in clear pavé set rhinestones. 2⅜" × 2¼".

figure 2.13 Wreath Fur Clip. Marked Eisenberg Original, c. 1940. Silver pot metal. Four uniquely cut clear rhinestones form the center with horizontal clear marquis-cut rhinestones forming the outer rim. Clear pavé set rhinestones form leaf designs throughout. Clear bezel sets add accent. 2½" × 2¾".

figure 2.14 Source unknown, c. 1941.

figure 2.15

figure 2.16

figure 2.17

Kamke's success with F&K led Eisenberg to use her designs exclusively. Her pieces were quickly acknowledged for their outstanding construction and use of colored stone. Eisenberg is said to have wanted to replicate the feel of the "crown jewels" and with some of their pieces they clearly showed that intention. Pearls were always a favorite and continued in the sterling period. Unique faux gray pearls matched Eisenberg's tailored wardrobes.

figure 2.15 Abstract Triangular Fur Clip. Marked Eisenberg Original, c. 1940. Silver pot metal done with a variety of stone cuts including pear, marquis, round, and oval in a variety of sizes. Line detailing and dimension is given with rows of clear pavé sets. 3⅛" × 3¾".

figure 2.16 Crystal Fur Clip. Marked Eisenberg Original, c. 1940. Silver pot metal holds bold and brilliant emerald and marquis cut clear stones surrounded and connected by varying sizes of clear bezel set rounds. 2" × 1¾".

figure 2.17 Crystal Dress Clip. Marked Script E, early 1940s. Silver pot metal. Two massive center teardrop clears are surrounded by large rectangular, square, and marquis-cut clear rhinestones. Bezel set clears add even more interest. 2½" × 1¾".

figure 2.19

figure 2.18

figure 2.18 Arched Dress Clip. Marked Eisenberg Original, late 1930s. Pot metal. Center arch is highlighted by two bezel-set clears framing the two large, clear, faceted pieces. Note that the two stones are different dimensions. 2¼" × ¾".

figure 2.19 Freeform Fur Clip. Marked Eisenberg Original, c. 1940. Art deco design. Oval clear rhinestones form a beautiful top "bud" design with pavé set clears streaming down and around. The strands are tipped with clear baguettes and one round. 3½" × 3½".

OPPOSITE ***figure 2.20*** From *Vogue*, February 1942.

figure 2.20
"Eisenberg Ice"
A
B
C
D
E
F
G
H
J
K
TO MELT HER HEART
To enthrall her . . . enslave her . . . reduce her resistance completely! On Valentine's Day. Crystal or colored stones, big and bright as a Sultan's treasure . . . designs as new and original as Eisenberg dresses. Each piece hallmarked Eisenberg Original and sold only at one leading store in your city.
Eisenberg Jewelry, Inc.
MERCHANDISE MART • CHICAGO
A. Companion clips, $15.00 a pair, $7.50 each
B. Spray clip, $12.50
C. Clip, $13.50
D. Bracelet, $14.50
E. Earrings, $3.75
F. Ring, $6.00
G. Compact, $12.50
H. Bowknot pin, $15.00
J. Clip, $20.00
K. Clip, $12.50
Design Patents Applied for

figure 2.21

figure 2.22

figure 2.24

figure 2.23 Floral Dress Clip. Marked Eisenberg Original, c. 1942. Half fan design of petals done in clear marquis stones framing a center oval rhinestone in amethyst. Bezel set clear accents run around the outside. 1½" × 1¾".

figure 2.21 Dimensional Deco Fur Clip. Marked Eisenberg Original, 1942. Crystal clears taper up and along as an outside row with a line running down the center. Stones are tilted along a slight arch. Channel set deep blue baguettes separate the clears. 2¾" × 2¼".

figure 2.22 Inverted Bouquet Fur Clip. Marked Eisenberg Original, patented 1942. Blooms are large, clear rounds done in a slightly arched design and accented with clear bezel sets. Stems are done with clear pavé sets and bound by a row of clear baguette stones. 4" × 2¼".

figure 2.24 Matching floral fur clips Marked Eisenberg Original, mid-1940s. Flowers flowing from stems in unique arrangements of clear bezel and pavé set stones. 2½" × 2½".

figure 2.25

figure 2.26

figure 2.27

figure 2.25 Elongated Fur Clip. Marked Eisenberg Original, c. 1942. Marquis clears frame a large oval clear with bezel-set clear accents. Above it, pavé ribbons frame a large emerald-cut clear. 2¾" × 1¾".

figure 2.26 Rhinestone Fur Clip. Marked Eisenberg Original, c. 1940. Silver pot metal. Clear stones in various cuts taper to a fan design done in pear shaped clears. Bezel set clears highlight the top and bottom of the piece. 3" × 2".

figure 2.27 Circular Rhinestone Brooch. Marked Eisenberg Original, c. 1942. Silver pot metal. Familiar center design of marquis clears framing a large oval, here encircled by clear pears along the bottom and marquis clears along the top. Bezel set clears are used throughout. Design is built up in the center. 3" diameter.

figure 2.28

figure 2.29

figure 2.30

figure 2.31

***figure* 2.28** Pearl and Rhinestone Fur Clip. Marked Eisenberg Original, c. 1940. Silver pot metal with antiqued patina and patterning. Faux pearl teardrops dangle along the bottom with round ones on the body. Large clears sparkle on top while a variety of bezel and pavé sets add accent. 3" × 2½".

***figure* 2.29** Pearl and Rhinestone Dress Clip. Marked Eisenberg Original, c. 1940. Silver pot metal. Seven faux pearl teardrops drape along the bottom. A half-moon of pear-shaped rhinestones surround a large faux pearl center stone. Bezel set clears complete the design. 2½" × 2½".

***figure* 2.30** Pearl and Rhinestone Fur Clip. Marked Eisenberg Original, c. 1940. Silver pot metal. Sweeping arms arch out to large center clear rhinestones with a dangling faux pearl teardrop. Pavé set stones cover the arms and body, and accent the huge bottom anchor stone. 2¾" × 2½".

***figure* 2.31** Pearl and Rhinestone Dress Clip. Marked Eisenberg Original, c. 1940. Unique treatment of the faux pearls that are "flocked" or coated. Large bright clears are outlined with the coated pearls that also dangle from the bottom. A truly different design. 2¼" × 2¼".

figure 2.32

figure 2.33

figure 2.32 Pearl lapel Pin, c. 1940. Same treatment of faux pearls that are flocked, or coated. This design was used at the same time as the pearl and rhinestone dress clip. 5" × 3".

figure 2.33 Pearl and Rhinestone Brooch. Marked Eisenberg Original and Sterling, mid-1940s. Abstract brooch of graduating faux white pearls swirling in loops interspersed and highlighted with lines of pavé set clears. 3" × 3".

figure 2.35

figure 2.34

figure 2.36

figure 2.34 Faux Pearl Fur Clip. Marked Eisenberg Original, c. 1940. Gold washed pot metal. Gorgeous gray faux pearls cluster in the body and are accented by four large unfoiled ruby stones with small bezel set clears. Large veined leaves and a stem lined with clears finish the design. 3" × 2¼".

figure 2.35 Pearl Fur Clip. Eisenberg Original Marked Eisenberg and Sterling, c. 1943. Four massive gray faux pearls tip the ends of a cornucopia design with the upward arching lines covered in clear pavé sets. Pearls are framed with sprigs of clear bezel set stones. 2¼" × 2¾".

figure 2.36 Pearl Earrings. Marked Block F & Sterling, c. 1943. Gray faux pearls are surrounded by clear bezel set rhinestones with clear pavé sets decorating the top. Often described as a cornucopia design. 1" × ¾".

Eisenberg loved to market Kamke's floral designs. Whether it was their clear rhinestones, Swarovski crystals, or vibrant colored stones, this jewelry was of the highest quality workmanship with unique and imaginative designs. Often these floral pieces were designed in a more abstract look. They were so popular that Eisenberg decided to market them in two varieties. Kamke's use of color was a new element of design for the company. In the 1930s, clear rhinestones and crystals were used predominantly. Kamke, however, wanted stones in seasonal colors and shades of nature. Blue in varying hues was a particular favorite.

figure 2.37

figure 2.38

figure 2.39

figure 2.40

figure 2.37 Vase of Flowers Fur Clip. Marked Eisenberg Original and Sterling, mid-1940s. Gold vermeil. Three pieces form this detailed bouquet in vase. Open-backed amethyst rhinestones of varying cuts form the vase and flowers. Gold leaves and clear pavé and bezel set accents. 4¼" × 2½".

figure 2.38 Basket Bouquet Brooch. Marked Eisenberg Original and Sterling, mid-1940s. Gold wash. Dimensional gold vase banded in tiny clears. Open-backed stones in a variety of colors and cuts. The outside blooms are interspersed with bezel set clears. Two pieces linked together. 2½" × 3".

figure 2.39 Agave Plant with Vase Brooch. Marked Eisenberg Original, c. 1940. Gold plated pot metal. Plant detailing is done with black enameling and yellow enameling covers the vase. Floral accent design is done with various cuts of colored stones around a center cabochon. 3½" × 2".

figure 2.40 Huge Stone Fur Clip. Marked Eisenberg Original and Sterling, mid-1940s. The centerpiece is a large, faceted, translucent citrine glass stone. 1½" × 1¼". Antiqued gold metal accented with black. The leaves and stems of this plum glitter with clear pavé set rhinestones. 2¾" × 2½".

figure 2.41

figure 2.42

figure 2.43

figure 2.44

figure 2.45 Huge Flower Bouquet. Marked Eisenberg Original, early 1940's. Copper patina over pot metal. Large, clear orange emerald-cut stones form flowers with bezel set pink crystals interspersed. Leaves and stems accented with green enamel and pavé set rhinestones. 4¾" × 2½".

figure 2.41 Large Leaf Stems Fur Clip. Marked Eisenberg Original with setters mark. Pot metal. Leaves detailed in green enamel surrounded by small pavé set rhinestones. Larger prong set rhinestones scattered around leaves. 3¼" × 3½".

figure 2.42 Ruth Kamke's Orchid. Marked Eisenberg Original and Sterling, c. 1943. A personal favorite of the designer and done in four colors. Bright citrine stones cluster to form the flower with bezel and pavé set clear accents. Dimensional leaves are highlighted with green enameling. 3¾" × 3¼".

figure 2.43 Pink Floral Brooch. Eisenberg Original Marked Eisenberg and Sterling, mid-1940s. Gold wash over sterling. Multi-hued pink blossoms in various sizes and cuts interspersed with bezel set clears. Golden leaves curl upward in layers and are anchored with one bottom pink accent stone. 3⅜" × 2¾".

figure 2.44 Vase with Flowers Brooch. Marked Eisenberg Original and Sterling, mid-1940s. Gold vermeil. A 1¼" citrine rhinestone forms the vase that holds topaz-colored rhinestone flowers and elaborate gold foliage, set with clear pavé rhinestones. 3⅞" × 2¾".

figure 2.46

figure 2.47

figure 2.48

figure 2.49

figure 2.46 Abstract Floral Fur Clip. Marked Eisenberg Original, c. 1940. Heavy gold wash over pot leaves curl about with bright oval and pear set clears tucked within. Bezel set accents are dotted about. 4" × 2½".

figure 2.47 Multi-Color Floral Brooch. Marked Eisenberg Original and Sterling, mid-1940s. Large, clear rounds are framed by petals with small colored rhinestones . The leaves and stems are covered with small clears with large colored stone pavé.

figure 2.48 Pink and Clear Floral Brooch. Marked with Script E, Early 1940s. Pot metal. Large faceted pink rhinestone petals frame clear pavé set flower with clear bezel set center accent. Pavé set clears decorate the leaves and stem. 3½" × 2¾".

figure 2.49 Daisy Fur Clip. Marked Eisenberg Original, advertised in *Women's Wear Daily* in 1939. Heavy gold wash over pot metal. White opalescent moonstones form the center flower. 41⁄8" × 3". *Courtesy of Jane Clarke, Morning Glory Antiques & Jewelry. www.MorningGloryAntiques.com.*

figure 2.50

figure 2.51

figure 2.52

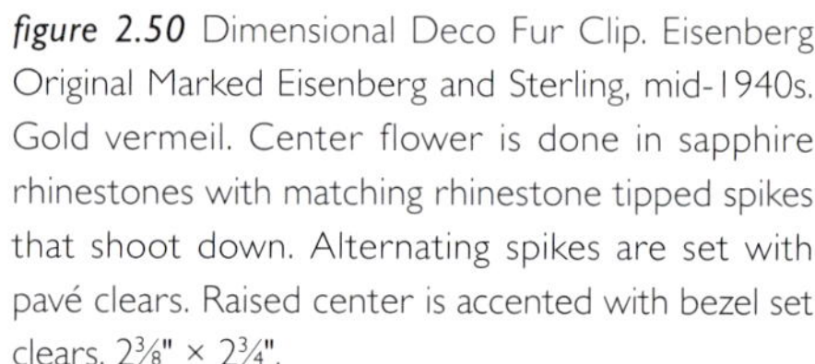

figure 2.50 Dimensional Deco Fur Clip. Eisenberg Original Marked Eisenberg and Sterling, mid-1940s. Gold vermeil. Center flower is done in sapphire rhinestones with matching rhinestone tipped spikes that shoot down. Alternating spikes are set with pavé clears. Raised center is accented with bezel set clears. 2⅜" × 2¾".

---

figure 2.51 Colorful Floral Fur Clip. Marked Eisenberg Original and Sterling, mid-1940s. Gold washed sterling in a freeform floral design. The colored stones are of different cuts and sizes but all are open-backed. Pavé set clears add touches of definition. 4" × 2½".

---

figure 2.52 Orchid Clip Earrings. Marked Script E and Sterling, c. 1948. Gold wash over sterling. Dimensional and curving petals with clear pavé set stones surrounding a deep blue center rhinestone. Clear rhinestones accent the outer curls of the top leaves. Incredibly realistic floral design. 1" × 1".

figure 2.53 *figure 2.54* *figure 2.55*

figure 2.56

figure 2.53 Amethyst Fur Clip. Marked Eisenberg Original and Sterling, mid-1940s. Gold wash. A huge faceted amethyst oval tops the piece with golden spikes dripping below, half of which are tipped with amethyst teardrops. 3" × 2½".

figure 2.54 Pink Floral Brooch. Eisenberg Original Marked Eisenberg and Sterling, mid-1940s. Gold wash over sterling. Multi-hued pink blossoms in various sizes and cuts interspersed with bezel-set clears. Golden leaves curl upward in layers and are anchored with one bottom pink accent stone. 3⅜" × 2¾".

figure 2.55 Abstract Fur Clip. Marked Eisenberg Original and Sterling, mid-1940s. Gold vermeil. Gorgeous pale yellow stones line the top section and run down the center of the bottom swirl. A thin line of clears frames the crosshatched top. 3½" × 2".

figure 2.56 Colorful Fur Clip. Marked Eisenberg Original and Sterling, mid-1940s. Gold wash. Top swirl is done with separated thin metal lines and is accented with a wide golden arc. The bottom fan has graduating colored rhinestones. Clear bezel set rhinestones decorate the fan tines. 3" × 3".

figure 2.57

figure 2.58

figure 2.59

figure 2.60

figure 2.57 Emerald Green Fur Clip. Marked Eisenberg Original & Sterling, c. 1941. A huge emerald stone anchors streamers of pavé set clears tipped with emerald marquis stones. Topped with a single row of clear pavé set stones. 2¼" × 1¾".

figure 2.58 Floral Fur Clip. Marked Eisenberg Original. Early 1940s. Gold wash over pot metal. Three gold buds with curving metal prongs are wrapped with pavé clears. Three large open petals hold various sized pink ovals with green enameled leaves finishing the design. 3¾" × 3¾".

figure 2.59 Floral Fur Clip. Marked Eisenberg Original, early 1940s. Three large clears are piled to form buds wrapped with pavé clears and decorated with small metal leaves. Three large open-work petals hold various clears sized with pavé-strewn leaves as accents. 3¾" × 3¾".

figure 2.60 Floral Dress Clip. Marked Eisenberg Original, late 1930s. Layered and curled gold petals surround a huge emerald center rhinestone. 2½" round with the center stone ⅞".

figure 2.61

figure 2.62

figure 2.63

figure 2.61 Flower Fur Clip. Marked Eisenberg Original, c. 1940. Gold plating over pot metal. Golden leaves and petals with emerald rhinestones in both marquis and diamond cut. Deep emerald oval center stone. Clear bezel sets add accents. 3⅜" × 2⅛".

figure 2.62 Golden King's Ransom Fur Clip. Marked Eisenberg Original, appears in ads in 1941. Gold pot metal. Rare occurrence of Eisenberg naming a piece. Floral design with curling petals. Large clear center stone surrounded by sapphire blue stones with sapphire petal accents. 3⅞" × 3½".

figure 2.63 Floral Fur Clip. Marked Eisenberg Original. A variation on the 1941 King's Ransom piece. Silver pot metal floral design with curling petals. Large clear rectangular center stone. Leaves are accented with pavé set clear stones. Bursting blooms are done with clear ovals. 3⅞" × 3½".

figure 2.64 Vogue, Dec. 1, 1937. Two patterned silk dresses, each with removable dress clips.

figure 2.66

figure 2.65

figure 2.65 Magenta Brooch. Marked Eisenberg Original, c. 1930s. Deco design is shown in the rows of magenta rounds and small florals done with small bezel set clears. Silver pot metal. 3⅛" × 1¾".

figure 2.66 Brooch. Marked Script E, c. 1940. Antiqued gold pot metal. Top ribbon work has clear pavé sets. Clear bezel sets form a center half circle and dot along the bottom. A bottom outer row is of oval shaped red rhinestones. 3⅜" × 3½".

figure 2.67 & figure 2.68

figure 2.67 Ruby Glass Brooch. Marked Eisenberg Original, late-1930s. Silver pot metal dangling dimensional ribbon design, half lined with small clear rhinestones. Bezel set clears and clear triangular stones ring the center ruby cabochon. 4" × 3".

figure 2.68 Side view showing the variety of shapes and depths of the translucent red stones held within the ribbons.

figure 2.69 *Vogue*. December 1, 1940.

figure 2.70

figure 2.71

figure 2.72

figure 2.73

figure 2.74 Pair of Matching Dress Clips. Marked Eisenberg Original, c. 1940. Silver pot metal highlights the sparkling clear rhinestones in various shapes. Deco lines are defined by clear pavé sets. A lot of detailing is present in these small clips. 1¾" × 1½".

figure 2.70 Topaz Fur Clip. Marked Eisenberg Original, 1940 ad. Gold wash pot metal. Large round topaz rhinestones form the design with the top anchor stones in oval and marquis cuts. Clear pavé set rhinestones, while clear bezel sets provide accent. 2¾" × 2¼".

figure 2.71 Topaz Fur Clip. Eisenberg Original Marked Eisenberg and Sterling, mid-1940s. Gold wash over sterling is beautifully shown in the open-work leaves. Large open-backed topaz teardrops drape down. One large, uniquely cut topaz rhinestone tops the piece with clear pavé sets providing design highlights. 3" × 2".

figure 2.72 Amber Accented Fur Clip. Marked Eisenberg Original, c. 1940. Gold wash pot metal. Clear rounds form three rows bracketed by rows of smaller horizontal emerald-cut amber stones. Clear bezel set stones frame the rows. 2¾" × 1¾".

figure 2.73 Pair of Amber Dress Clips. Marked Eisenberg Original, c. 1940. Heavy gold washed pot metal holds bright amber stones of various shapes. Clear pavé sets around the amber stones. 1¾" × 1¼".

figure 2.75 Art Deco Brooch. Marked Eisenberg Original, mid- to late-1930s. Art Deco styling in silver pot metal with tiny clear rhinestones. Open work highlights the center row of three large cut topaz stones outlined with cut emerald-green stones. 1⅞" × 3⅝".

figure 2.75

figure 2.76 *Vogue*—c. 1940.

figure 2.77

figure 2.78

figure 2.79

figure 2.80

figure 2.77 Elongated Fur Clip. Marked Eisenberg Original, 1940 ad. Silver pot metal with all clear rhinestones in large emerald, oval, and marquis cuts. Curved lines and dotted accents of clear bezel set rhinestones finish the piece. 3¼" × 1½".

figure 2.78 Dimensional Floral Dress Clip. Marked Eisenberg Original, c. 1940. Silver pot metal. The flower is formed with three layers of marquis cut clears surrounding a clear round. The stem and leaves are covered with pavé set clears and are accented with several large clears. 3½" × 2".

figure 2.79 Huge Floral Fur Clip. Marked Eisenberg Original, 1941 ad. Silver pot metal. Clear rhinestones accented with pavé and bezel set rounds. 3¾"× 2".

figure 2.80 Floral Fur Clip. Marked Eisenberg Original, c. 1940. Silver pot metal flower formed with layers of clear, open-backed stones. A large stem frames the side of the veins and the leaves. 3⅝" × 3".

figure 2.81

figure 2.82

figure 2.83

figure 2.84

figure 2.81 Snowflake Brooch. Marked Script E and Sterling, mid-1940s. Snowflake design is done with clear round, marquis, and oval rhinestones. Bezel set clears ring the outside and accent the center.

figure 2.82 Fascinating Floral Fur Clip. Eisenberg Original Marked Eisenberg and Sterling, mid-1940s. Free form lines dotted with clear rhinestones form the rings of petals surrounding the clear center. al. Draping buds are done with triangular clear rhinestones in two sizes with clear rhinestones outlining them. 3" × 2½".

figure 2.83 Fur Clip Leaf with Latticework.. Marked Eisenberg and Sterling, mid-1940s. Large crosshatched petals are centered by large clear squares surrounded by bezel set clears. The center vein is lined with graduating clears. 4" × 2½".

figure 2.84 Sterling Floral Brooch. Marked Eisenberg Original and Sterling, c. 1943. Unique brooch with open weave leaves outlined with clear rhinestones. Deep emerald-green stones form the floral center and bottom sprig, which is veined in clears. 3½" × 3½". *From the collection of Barbara Jones.*

Eisenberg also introduced dangling fur clips that were heavy and colorful. Molded glass and faux turquoise made these fur clips very popular, and today they are exceptionally rare. Many did not bear the Eisenberg Original mark and created an authenticity problem similar to what occurred years before.

figure 2.85

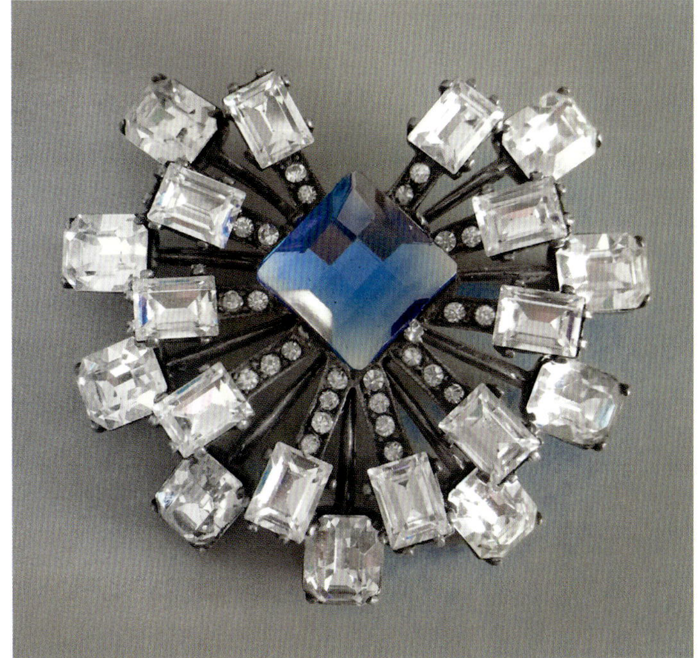

figure 2.86

figure 2.85 Aqua Tri-Feather Fur Clip. Marked Eisenberg Original, early 1940s. Pot metal. An impressive forty-one stones of tapering sizes form the three curling feathers. Clear pavé set stones vein each feather and run along the elaborate bottom bow. 4" × 3 ⅝".

figure 2.86 Unusual Brooch. Marked Script E, early 1940s. Silver pot metal. Layers faceted with colored center blue stone that anchors the piece. Two spokes fan out, each tipped with a clear faceted rhinestone. 2⅓". *Courtesy of Jane Clarke, Morning Glory Antiques & Jewelry. www.MorningGloryAntiques.com*

figure 2.87

figure 2.88

figure 2.89

figure 2.90

figure 2.87 Stunning Fur Clip. Marked Eisenberg Original, c. 1940. Massive blue glass open-backed stone "drop" at the bottom. Above that are pavé and bezel set clear ribbons highlighted by five smaller blue glass open-backed stones. 3" × 2¼".

figure 2.88 Abstract Sapphire Fur Clip. Marked Eisenberg Original Sterling, c. mid-1940s. Three four-sided clear sapphire glass stones with gold tone and pavé set stones forming petals of a flower with seven spikes emerging. 3¼" × 2¾".

figure 2.89 Rare Victorian Inspired Brooch. Marked Eisenberg, late 1930s. Top bar pin holds a clear emerald-cut flanked by two uniquely cut pale blue stones. Bottom pendant is centered with a huge open-backed faceted stone framed by pale blue pears. Clear bezel sets add accent. 3¼" × 2".

figure 2.90 Aqua Dress Clip. Marked Eisenberg Original, late 1930s. Three lines of stones showcase the magnificent sparkle of the large aqua faceted stones. Clear bezel sets outline each large aqua setting. 2¾" × 1⅝".

figure 2.91

figure 2.92

figure 2.93

figure 2.94

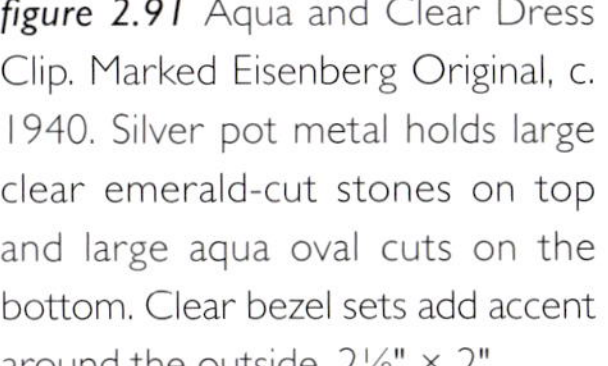

figure 2.91 Aqua and Clear Dress Clip. Marked Eisenberg Original, c. 1940. Silver pot metal holds large clear emerald-cut stones on top and large aqua oval cuts on the bottom. Clear bezel sets add accent around the outside. $2\frac{1}{8}$" × 2".

figure 2.92 Aqua Rhinestone Brooch. Marked Eisenberg Original, c. 1940. Antique gold pot metal. Swirling lines set with small clear rhinestones define the design. Aqua stones in many cuts and sizes are showcased. $3\frac{1}{2}$" × $3\frac{1}{4}$".

figure 2.93 Unusual Dress Clip. Marked Eisenberg Original, c. 1930s. Pot Metal. Red, green, and blue rhinestones are showcased in the top piece with two rows of ovals and a line of emerald-cuts with clear bezel set accents. Irregular colored glass bead dangles. 3" × $2\frac{1}{2}$".

figure 2.94 Articulated Dress Clip. Marked Eisenberg Original, c. 1930s. Molded floral detailing in antiqued gold pot metal forms the base and flower drops. Bezel set clears center the flowers. Aqua rhinestones top the piece with aqua glass beads dangling from each flower. $4\frac{1}{2}$" × 3".

figure 2.95

figure 2.96

figure 2.95 Matching Fur Clips. Marked Eisenberg Original, c. 1940. Gold wash over pot metal. Beautiful curved pieces done with clear pavé set rhinestones outlined with round aqua rhinestones. Two strands of gold weave through the designs. 1¾" × 1½".

figure 2.96 Aqua Fur Clip. Marked Eisenberg Original and Sterling, mid-1940s. Gold vermeil over sterling. Large aqua rhinestones in oval and round cuts give the piece its color. Clear bezel set stones accent the bottom while clear pavé sets highlight the scrollwork. 3" × 2½".

figure 2.97

figure 2.98

figure 2.99

figure 2.97 Green Fruit Salad Dress Clip. Marked Eisenberg Original, c. 1930s. Deep emerald-green molded glass stones form the base with three dangling green "melon balls." Clear bezel set rhinestones finish the design. 2" × 2⅞".

figure 2.98 This piece is missing its dangles, but shows a variation of the rare molded glass stones. Marked Eisenberg Original, c. 1930s. 1⅝" × 2".

figure 2.99 Faux Turquoise Dress Clip. Unmarked, c. 1930s. Gold pot metal frames molded faux turquoise glass stones with three dangling faux turquoise drops. Bezel set clear rhinestones add accent. 2" × 2⅛".

figure 2.100

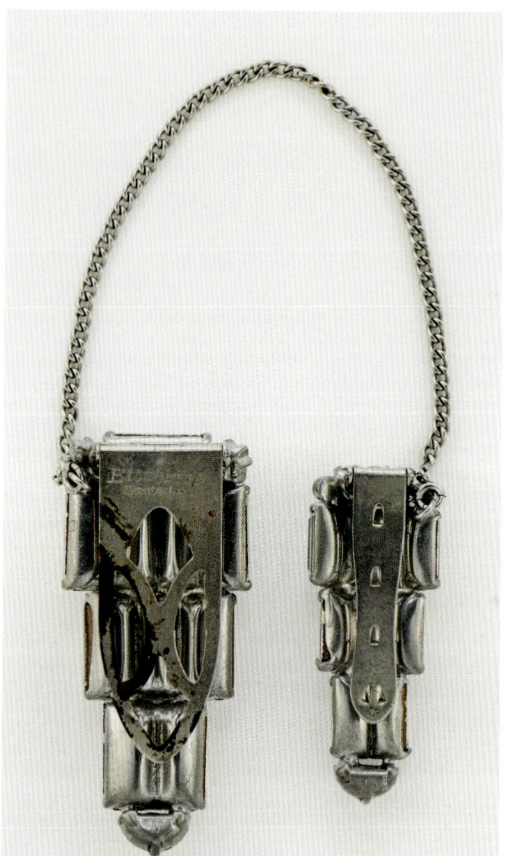

figure 2.101

figure 2.102

figure 2.100 Dress Clip Pair. Marked Eisenberg Original, early 1940s. Silver pot metal. Each is done with three stacked rows of clear baguettes, though their top rows are slightly different. Both are tipped at the bottom by large clear ovals. Large 2½" × 1⅛". Small 2" × ¾".

figure 2.101 These pieces are linked by a silver pot metal chain. The large piece bears the traditional marked Eisenberg Original dress clip back while the smaller piece has a thinner unmarked variation.

figure 2.102 Dimensional Deco Dress Clip. Marked Eisenberg Original, early 1940s. Silver pot metal. Top row of oval and pear clears with clear bezel accents. Two rows of emerald-cut clears and two rows of clear baguettes form the body. Tipped at bottom by an oval clear. 3¼" × 1¾".

figure 2.103

figure 2.104

figure 2.105

figure 2.106

figure 2.103 Early Originals Dress Clip. Marked Eisenberg Original, c. 1930s. Antiqued gold pot metal is accented by faux turquoise beads and red faceted crystals. Center pinwheel design. 2½" × 1¾".

figure 2.104 Linked Dress Adornments. Unmarked, c. 1930s. These pinwheel sew-ons mirror the dress clip they were found with in metal, stones, and crystals, and even have a stone setter's mark, but, sadly, they aren't marked for Eisenberg and can't be verified. Connected by a heavy link chain.

figure 2.105 Blue and Coral Bowtie Brooch. Marked Eisenberg Original, c. 1930s. Gold wash pot metal. Open-backed blue stones of various cuts and sizes decorate the ribbons with a center knot of tiny faux coral beads. 1¾" × 3". *From the Collection of Joanna van Ritbergen.*

figure 2.106 Orchid Fur Clip. Marked Eisenberg Original, c. 1930s. Antiqued gold pot metal. Five large faceted aqua stones are surrounded by petals of tiny red cranberry glass stones. 2¾" × 2". *Courtesy of Jane Clarke, Morning Glory Antiques & Jewelry, www.MorningGloryAntiques.com.*

figure 2.107

figure 2.108

figure 2.109

figure 2.107 Brooch. Marked Eisenberg Original, c. 1930s. Silver pot metal. Large rectangular and triangular marcasites are prong set with pavé lines of small rounds. Orange cabochons form the center, fan the edges, and add accent. Blue rhinestones of differing cuts and sizes. 2¼" × 3½".

figure 2.108 Art Deco Fur Clip. Marked Eisenberg Original, c. 1930s. Antiqued gold patina pot metal accented with black detailing. A twisted metal rope frames a large center open-backed blue stone. Small faux coral beads dot the "wings" of this unique piece. 1½" × 2½".

figure 2.109 Unusual four-leaf-clover-shaped brooch. Marked Eisenberg Original with setters mark, early 1940s. Pot metal. Pear-shaped, topaz-colored stones form inside of each leaf surrounded by faux turquoise stones. Center is marquis-shaped, topaz-colored stones with bezel set clear rhinestones. Accents of topaz rhinestones and turquoise around leaves. 2¾" × 2⅛".

figure 2.110 Striking Dress Clip. Marked Eisenberg Original, c. 1930s. Silver pot metal centered with a large blue faceted glass open-backed stone. Bezel set clear stones in heavy settings along with multi-colored glass beads decorate the rest of the piece. 1½" × 1¾".

figure 2.111 Aqua and turquoise clear rhinestone fur clip. Marked Eisenberg Original, late 1930s. Antique gold pot metal. Abstract shape. Seven aqua colored clear round stones and three turquoise colored clear emerald-shaped stones. All prongs set. Scattered different colored cabochon stones. 2¼" × 2¼".

figure 2.112

figure 2.113

figure 2.114

figure 2.115

figure 2.112 Multi-Color Dress Clip. Marked Eisenberg Original, c. 1930s. A many-hued delight of colored rhinestones and small colored bead accents. Open spaces and clear accents along the top finish off this vivid piece. Pot metal. 2¾" × 2½".

figure 2.113 Aqua and Pink Fur Clip. Marked Eisenberg Original, c. 1940s. Silver pot metal. Small floral vignettes are formed by massive pink and aqua stones framed by clear rhinestones. 4" × 2".

figure 2.114 Gemstone Dress Clip. Marked Eisenberg Original, c. 1930s. Patterned, antiqued gold pieces are layered around a 1½" faux turquoise stone, with a small faux turquoise nugget dangling at center bottom. Imitation mineral nuggets done with glass stones of multiple colors hang from the layered pieces. 2¾" × 1½".

figure 2.115 Unusual Dangling Dress Clip. Marked Eisenberg Original, c. 1930s. Unique glass patterned drops in pink, aqua, blue, and green hang from an antiqued patina link chain along with faux turquoise stones and imitation pearls. 4¼" × 2¼".

Bracelets were a substantial part of the company's work. Hinged bracelets are rare across all the decades. The gold tone bracelet is the only one we have ever seen.

figure 2.116

figure 2.117

figure 2.116 Hinged Bracelet. Marked Block Eisenberg, c. 1950s. Rhodium. The bracelet is four rows of linked rounds set at slightly different angles that flare out into a huge oval front design featuring two large pear-shaped clear stones set within. 8½" × 1½". *From the Collection of Laura Sutton.*

figure 2.117 Glamour Bracelet. Marked Block E, c. 1950s. Stunning clear rhinestone hinged and domed bracelet. Rhodium. Two petal-shaped pieces set with clear rhinestones form arched panels with open spaces creating dimension. A row of clear round rhinestones runs down the center. *Courtesy of the Erin Byrne Buffaline Collection.*

figure 2.118

figure 2.119

figure 2.120

figure 2.118 Rare Gold Originals Cuff. Marked Eisenberg Original, c. 1940. Heavy gold wash over pot metal. Massive front decoration of five textured rows—three rows of waves and two of chain link. Bracelet makes a bold statement. 8½" × 1½".

figure 2.119 Eisenberg Original mark on hinged cuff bracelet. Original safety chain remains.

figure 2.120 The weighty, pot metal base of this bracelet, the very small interior dimension, and the correct mark do seem to confirm that this is a rare, early non-rhinestone Original bracelet.

figure 2.121

figure 2.122

figure 2.123

figure 2.124

figure 2.121 Source unknown, c. 1942.

figure 2.122 Emerald and Clear Stone Bracelet. Marked Eisenberg Original, ad, c. 1942. Gold pot metal. Large emerald-cut clear and green center stones are linked by two small round and one square bezel set clears. 7½" × ⅝".

figure 2.123 Pink and Gold Bracelet. Marked Script E and Sterling, c. 1946. Vermeil. Part of a parure advertised in 1946, the brooch is also shown here. Elaborate gold metal links are accented with clear rhinestones and are centered by large pink ovals. 7¼" × ½".

figure 2.124 Articulated Brooch. Eisenberg Original. Marked Eisenberg and Sterling. Additionally marked E on each piece. Appears in advertising in 1946. Gold vermeil. Looping ribbon design with jointed dangling floral vines holding pink oval stones. Both bezel and pavé set clear rhinestone accents. 2½" × 2½ ". *From a Private Collection.*

figure 2.125 Choker Demi-Parure. Marked Block E, late 1940s. Choker done with three rows of linked golden balls. Necklace has safety chain. Matching gold ball earrings are clip. Necklace 15" × 1". Earrings ¾".

figure 2.126

figure 2.127

Though done mostly in the later "Ice" period, the 1950s would see a demand for matched jewelry pieces. It appears Eisenberg offered many designs in a variety of set arrangements. Many were also offered individually allowing the buyer to customize their demi or full parure.

figure 2.126 Demi-Parure Necklace and Bracelet. Marked Eisenberg, late 1940s. Rhodium. Ivory pearls in one row with rhinestones on either side of pearls. Crisscross design holds rows together. Necklace (50 pearls, 102 rhinestones), 15" long. Bracelet (25 pearls, 52 rhinestones), 7" long.

figure 2.127 Amethyst Bracelet. Marked Eisenberg Original and Sterling, mid-1940s. The seven segments are done with large emerald-cut amethyst stones surrounded by clear bezel sets. Sterling bars that mimic the clasp link the segments. 7⅝" × ½".

The Sweet Smell of Success

Eisenberg's Fragrances

With the new jewelry line flourishing and the clothing line continuing to grow, Eisenberg & Sons added a cosmetics division in 1938. The company's first fragrance was "847" and was packaged in a frosted lady figurine.

In 1937 Eisenberg outgrew its location at 309 West Jackson Boulevard and leased a much larger space down the street at 847 West Jackson. The advertisement launching "847" claimed that numbers "have numerological power," but it is far more likely that the name

figure 3.1

figure 3.3

figure 3.2

figure 3.1 Mademoiselle Magazine, 1940. *From the Collection of Laura Sutton.*

figure 3.2 Figural Lady Bottle. Not marked. Bottle would have come in a blue velvet presentation box. Bottle was available for the whole life of the fragrances. Variations of the bottle were used across all the product lines. 3½" × 2¼".

figure 3.3 *Vogue*. Dec 1, 1940. One of the first advertisements that showcases clothing, jewelry, and perfume. It lists Eisenberg & Sons as only dressmakers and jewelers, even though it spotlights their second perfume. It also pre-dates the official formation of Eisenberg Jewelry and advertises that they were selling more than just dress and fur clips.

came from the new address, a nod to the company's success. Future fragrances would thankfully have more alluring names.

The "847" fragrance came in two sizes priced at $25 for the large and $7.50 for the small. A non-figural option for your purse was a pricey $2.50. There were two versions of "847": "847" A, the exotic, and "847" B, the delicate. An eau de cologne, "Aromique 847," also came in two sizes.

About this time, a woman in a billowing skirt and an off-the-shoulder gown became the signature image for a cosmetics division, though the glass ball she held sometimes transformed into a bouquet. She also started to appear on the clothing labels, but with her hands on her skirt.

The frosted figurine bottle lasted through the line's lifetime, though she has rarely been found in the lovely blue velvet box that was her original packaging.

Interestingly, though the cosmetics division is listed on the introductory ads for "847", subsequent ads refer only to the company as perfumers. No mention was made of the jewelry line Eisenberg had recently launched.

During this period, many well-respected labels were also stepping into the world of perfume. In *Perfume, Cologne, and Scent Bottles* Jacquelyne North states, "The 1930s in America saw many cosmetic firms and couture houses introducing perfumes."[1] Eisenberg would follow the lead of other American labels and journey to France for their fragrances.

In 1940 they would leave "847" behind and begin advertising a fragrance named Excitement.

After four-and-a-half years at 847 Jackson Boulevard, Eisenberg expanded into the massive Merchandise Mart complex, thirty percent larger than the previous location.

A photo postcard of the Merchandise Mart contains the following information: "World's largest building located on North Bank Drive and Wells Street, is a 'Wholesale City under one roof.' It houses several hundred wholesale mercantile concerns representing 'Chicago, the Great Central Market.' Built in 1930 by Marshall Field & Co. at a cost of over 30 million dollars."

figure 3.4 Postcard of Merchandise Mart.

figure 3.5 Back of postcard.

figure 3.6 Eisenberg Shop in Chicago, Illinois, November 19, 1941.
Chicago History Museum. HB-06763-A. *Photo by Hedrich-Blessing.*

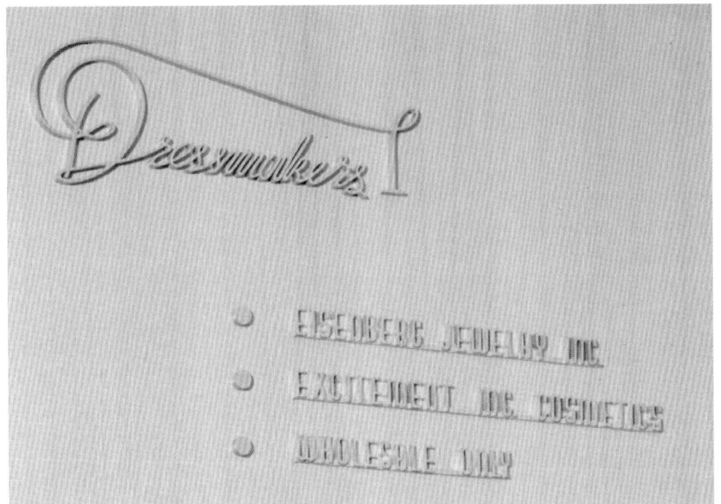

figure 3.7

In 1941 Eisenberg & Sons still considered themselves "dressmakers" first, but their name on the Merchandise Mart building included all three divisions in the only listing we found identifying the cosmetic division as Excitement Inc. Cosmetics.

The new location offered buyers a truly remarkable experience. It had a grand, picture-framed stage in an oval showroom for fashion viewings. One wall of the reception room featured three-dimensional white appliqués of the company's signature figural lady. Perfumes had their own showroom that included a display case for accessories and jewelry.

figure 3.8

figure 3.7 Eisenberg Shop in Chicago, November 19, 1941. Chicago History Museum. Close-up from HB-06763-A. *Photo by Hedrich-Blessing.*

figure 3.8 Eisenberg Shop in Chicago, November 19, 1941. Chicago History Museum. HB-06763-C. *Photo by Hedrich-Blessing.*

figure 3.9

figure 3.10

By 1943 Eisenberg introduced two fragrances—Stirring and Startling—in addition to the existing Excitement. Excitement's fragrance was advertised as fresh and buoyant, Stirring was said to be light and nostalgic, while Startling was tagged as heady and dramatic. There would be full lines for all three fragrances including sachets, soaps, and powders.

figure 3.11

figure 3.12

figure 3.9 Eisenberg Shop in Chicago, November 19, 1941. Chicago History Museum. Close-up from HB-06763-C. Perfume Niche. *Photo by Hedrich-Blessing.*

figure 3.10 Eisenberg Shop in Chicago, November 19, 1941. Chicago History Museum. Close-up from HB-06763-C. Display Case. *Photo by Hedrich-Blessing.*

figure 3.11 Eisenberg Cologne Sachet. For the Stirring fragrance. Images of the figural lady hand the top. 1 oz. size. 3¾" × 1¾".

figure 3.12 *Good Housekeeping*, October 1945.

figure 3.13 Source unknown, c. 1944. *From the Collection of Laura Sutton.*

figure 3.14

figure 3.15

figure 3.14 *Eisenberg & Sons* catalog, copyright 1944. Stirring, Startling, and Excitement scents in various packaging. Lipstick and powder also displayed. *Courtesy of D. Brett Benson, Inc. West Palm Beach, FL.*

figure 3.15 Celluloid lipstick case with metal base. The signature Eisenberg figural lady is raised on top. $2\frac{1}{4}$" × $\frac{3}{4}$".

OPPOSITE
figure 3.16 *Vogue*. August 15, 1943. Offered in light, medium, and dark.

Eisenberg Originals
EXCITEMENT LIPSTICK . . . lingering on your lips
as a challenge to adventure . . . thrilling as
your first kiss. In Medium, Light or Dark.
EISENBERG ICE . . . lapel pin bespangled with fiery,
brilliantly-cut stones set by hand. Crystal
stones in sterling silver. Colored stones
in gold-finish sterling silver.
Excitement
LIPSTICK BY EISENBERG
EISENBERG & SONS • DRESSMAKERS • PERFUMERS • JEWELERS
MERCHANDISE MART, CHICAGO, ILL.

figure 3.16

figure 3.17 Source unknown, 1940s. Two-page ad indicates that this was part of the Eisenberg Originals line picturing two of the older enticing bottles and two of the celluloid lipstick cases with metal base. The signature figural lady is raised on top. *From the Collection of Laura Sutton.*

figure 3.18 Source unknown, 1940s.
From the Collection of Laura Sutton.`

figure 3.19 *Vogue*, 1948. When Enticing was launched it was advertised with the old style packaging. About this time, Eisenberg revamped the packaging to include the bold E design.

figure 3.20 *Vogue, 1948. From the Collection of Laura Sutton.*

figure 3.21 Trio of Eisenberg Perfume Bottles with Box. Box Marked Perfume Cologne by Eisenberg with bold E design in gold and light gray. Bottles all bear the bold gold E and are all Excitement by Eisenberg. Large $4\frac{3}{4}$" × $1\frac{7}{8}$". Small $2\frac{3}{4}$" × $\frac{7}{8}$".

figure 3.21

New!
A PERFUMED LIPSTICK
EISENBERG
SUBURBAN
VIBRANT COLOR . . .
LILTING FRAGRANCE . . .
NEW ENCHANTMENT FOR YOUR LIPS!
SUBURBAN RED PERFUMED LIPSTICK, $1.50
IN MATCHING FRAGRANCE . . .
SUBURBAN COLOGNE, $2.50
SUBURBAN PERFUME STICK, $1.50
PRICES PLUS TAX
AT SMART STORES, OR ORDER FROM
EISENBERG & SONS
MERCHANDISE MART • CHICAGO 54
DRESSMAKERS • JEWELERS • PERFUMERS

By 1943, Eisenberg was also advertising lipstick. In 1947 the company offered five lipstick colors, each one scented with Excitement perfume. Solid perfume sticks were on offer for all four fragrances. That year Eisenberg also launched its fifth fragrance, Enticing, a scent advertised as piquant and provocative.

figure 3.23

figure 3.24

figure 3.25

figure 3.26

Eisenberg had only two labels other than Originals over the years: Suwanee Ensembles was exclusively for clothing, and the Suburban line, launched in 1949, cut across fashion, jewelry, and fragrance. Suburban fragrance appeared in *Vogue* in April 1949.

Eisenberg continued to offer all of its fragrances into the 1950s, except for "847", which had been laid to rest with the introduction of Excitement. The last Eisenberg fragrance ad we found in *Vogue* was in 1952.

figure 3.23 Gift Box of Perfumes. Marked Fascination Quartet and Perfume Colognes by Eisenberg, c. 1950s.

figure 3.24 Fascination Quartet Bottles. Each bottle has the bold E and fragrance name. Each is five ounces. Fragrances are Excitement, Stirring, Startling, and Suburban.

figure 3.25 Purse Fragrance Bottles. Both are marked Excitement by Eisenberg, c. 1940s. The skinny one is glass with a gold outer layer and is 1⅞" × ¾". The round one is glass with shiny gold discs affixed to the front and rear and is 1½" × 2".

figure 3.26 Stirring Perfume Bottle in original box, mid-1940s. Cream and light blue with the fragrance's moniker in a black wavy label. The design was used in the 1940s. Box is 2⅛" × 2".

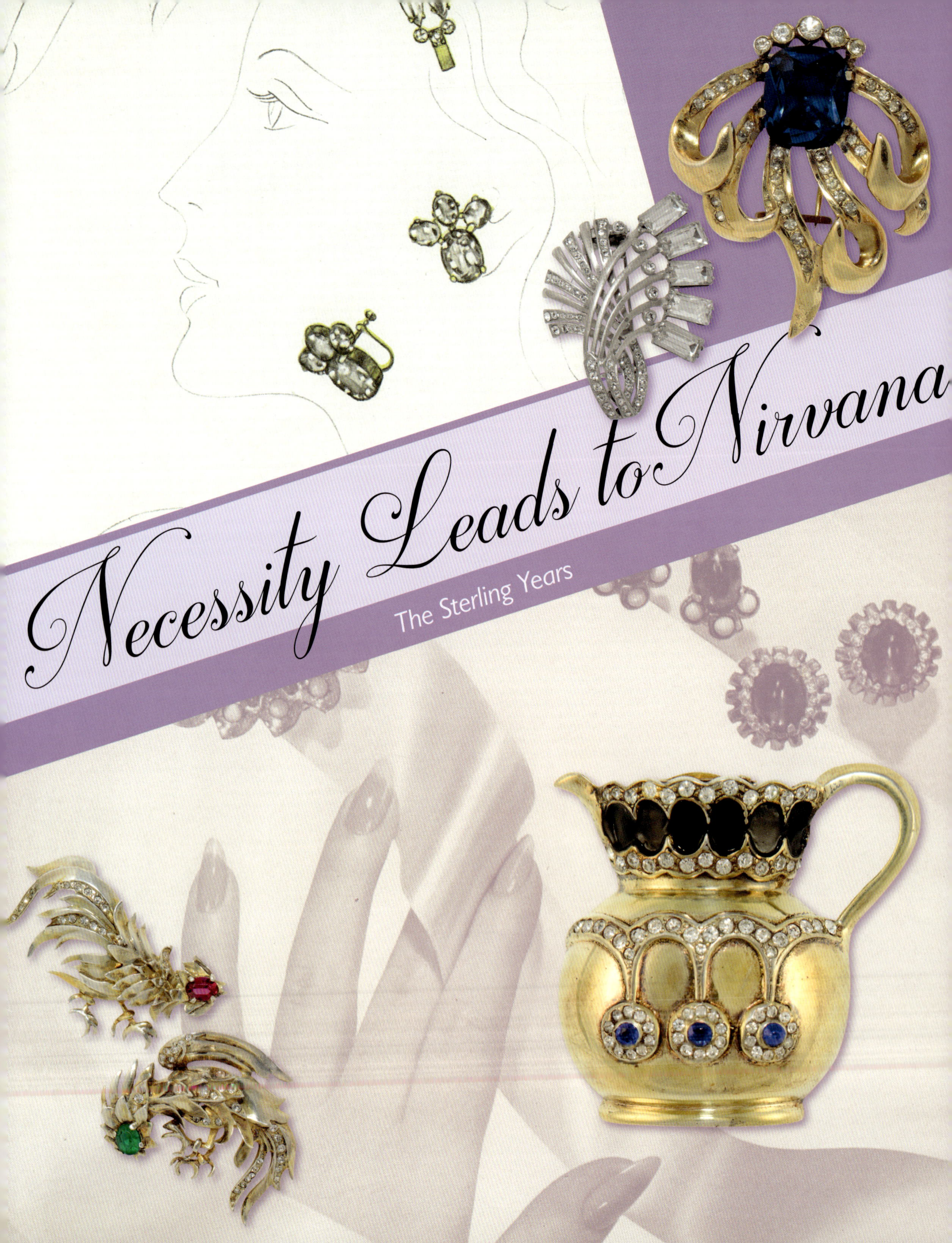
Necessity Leads to Nirvana
The Sterling Years

Facing a pot metal shortgage during WWII, costume jewelers had to find a substitute material, and this led to the use of sterling. It seems that all pieces commissioned from F&K prior to their exclusivity contract with Eisenberg had to be purchased in at least a gross, or 144 pieces. Given the rarity of some of the Eisenberg designs, one wonders if the minimum order was strictly enforced, especially for some of the more complicated Original pieces. Surely there was a contract regarding collection sizes, for F&K continued to operate profitably with its one client.

As F&K's primary designer, Ruth Kamke was extremely talented at designing pieces that could be molded and manufactured for a reasonable cost.

No one would have guessed that these sterling pieces would become the most valuable of Eisenberg pieces. The change to sterling may have been done out of necessity, but these pieces are treasured now.

Soon the flow of crystals and rhinestones from Europe also dried up, and stockpiles in the tightly packed Rhode Island warehouses were depleted. During this period Eisenberg's designs were made with "American ice," a form of pressed glass, rather than the machine-cut, high-lead-content imports. These stones lacked the reflectivity of the European beauties, and F&K removed the foil backings to try to "lighten" and enhance them.

Using rhodium instead of sterling, similar themes emerged. For the second time in Eisenberg's history, "Ice" was now designated a specific line of jewelry. The stones were clear with a crystalline shade of blue. Bows began to appear again, sometimes using Brazilian topaz. Floral designs dominated Kamke's new line. An unusual collection of red cabochons and turquoise stones were advertised at Christmas 1944. Unique red glass stones and faux turquoise beads were available in brooches, bracelets, and earrings.

figure 4.1 Sinbad Fur Clip. Marked Eisenberg Original, c. 1940. Gold plated. Figural of a turbaned head with seven dangling strands of multi-colored teardrop rhinestones. Clear rhinestones additionally decorate the turban while blue and black enameling adds dimension. Sinbad is the name given by collectors. 3¼" × 2".

figure 4.2 Figural Fur Clip. Marked Eisenberg Original, c. 1940. Gold plated. Male figure wearing elaborate garb and tiny green stone earring. Often called the Egyptian, he holds an immense cornucopia. Deep green round rhinestones form flowers. 4" x 1¾".

figure 4.3

figure 4.4

figure 4.5

figure 4.6

figure 4.3 Two-Tone Figural Fur Clip. Marked Eisenberg Original, late 1930s. Called either the Angel or the Cherub. The body is gold plate over pot metal while the wings are silver pot metal. Clear rhinestones cover the wings and are bezel set above the head. 3¼" × 2¾".

figure 4.4 Stardust Bow Brooch. Marked Eisenberg Original, late 1930s. Gold wash. Scalloped edge bow is centered by a 1" faceted aqua stone. The ribbon loops are decorated with incised stars, each centered by a clear rhinestone. Pavé clears run along several ribbon sections. 2" × 3¾".

figure 4.5 Abstract Fur Clip. Marked Eisenberg Original, early 1940s. Gold washed pot metal (not the usual sterling). Ruth Kamke says this is not a torso, as it is often called. Darker veining around the faux turquoise bead lines. A clear round sits on top with an aqua oval at the bottom. 2¼" × 2¼".

figure 4.6 Asian Mask Fur Clip. Marked Eisenberg Original, c. 1940. Gold plated. Dimensional face is accented with clear rhinestones with a large clear stone on top of head. Has ten dangling fringe lines of eighteen emerald open-backed rhinestones, each finished with a gold bead drop. 4½" × 2".

figure 4.7

figure 4.8

figure 4.7 Pitcher Fur Clip. Marked Eisenberg Original and Sterling, advertised Christmas 1944. Gold vermeil with black enameling detail at top outlined with tiny clears. Tiny clears also decorate the body and encircle three small blue rhinestone accents. 2" × 2".

figure 4.8 Abstract Spider Fur Clip. Eisenberg Original Marked Eisenberg and Sterling, mid-1940s. Dimensional open-work legs are tipped with clear rhinestones that also cover the head. The body is a uniquely cut, faceted blue rhinestone. Collectors named it Spider. 3" × 2".

figure 4.9

Eisenberg Ice*
Fabulous as fashion's richest mood,
sparkling as Springtime.
Crystal clear imported stones hand-set
with precious care in sterling silver.
EISENBERG JEWELRY INC.
Merchandise Mart, Chicago 54, Ill.

*Reg. U. S. Pat. Off.

figure 4.10

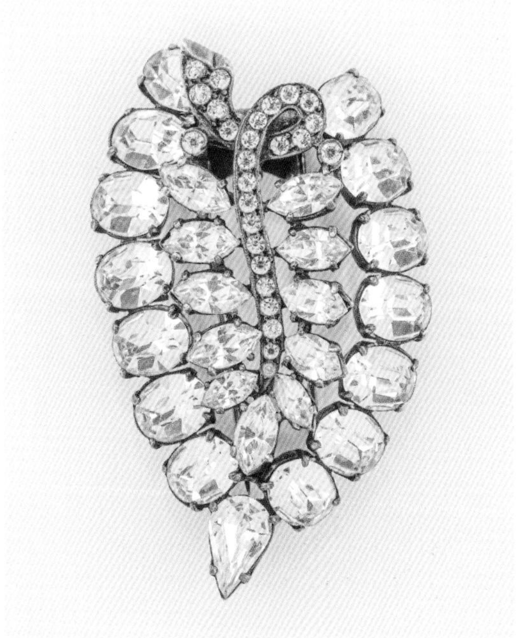

figure 4.11

figure 4.12

OPPOSITE
figure 4.9 *Vogue*, February 1, 1948.

figure 4.10 Elaborate Floral Brooch. Marked Eisenberg Original and Sterling, mid-1940s. Flowers are formed with large round clears and groupings of smaller bezel set clears. Leaves are solid sterling or set with tiny clears. Center stems are highlighted with clears.

figure 4.11 Stylized Leaf Fur Clip. Eisenberg Original Marked Eisenberg and Sterling, c. 1943. Layering and open areas create dimension. Oval clears create the outside row, with marquis clears forming the inner. Clear pavé sets line the vein. 2¾" × 1¾".

figure 4.12 Pair of Brooches. Marked Eisenberg Original and Sterling, mid-1940s. Flowers are formed with graduated clear round rhinestones both bezel and prong set. Clear pavé sets run along the leaf and stems. Bouquets are banded in a thick ring with a large clear triangular rhinestone. 2¼" × 1¼".

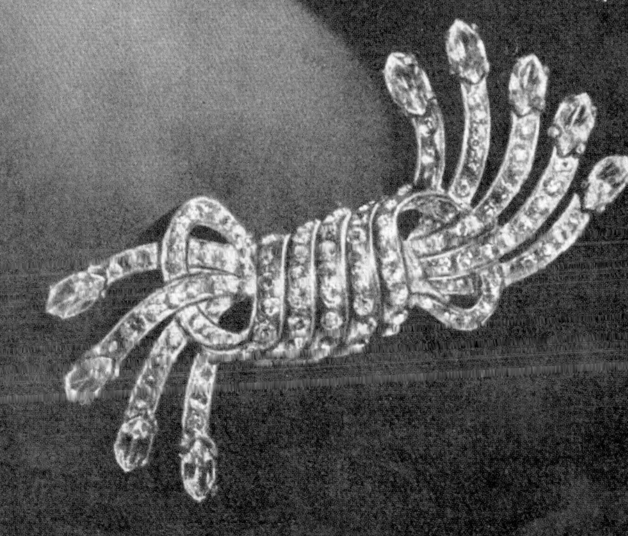

figure 4.13 *Vogue*, March 15, 1946.

figure 4.14

figure 4.15

figure 4.16

figure 4.14 Clear Articulated Brooch. Eisenberg Original Marked Eisenberg & Sterling, advertised in 1946. Free swinging pendant has a large pear-shaped stone with bezel and pavé set rhinestones ringing it. Pavé set swirls lead to a large center oval stone ringed in bezel set rounds. 3" × 1⅜".

figure 4.15 Abstract Floral Fur Clip. Marked Eisenberg Original and Sterling, mid-1940s. Two large faceted rectangular stones anchor the piece with clear pavé lined leaves. Marquis-cut clear stones of various sizes drape down and bezel set clears provide accent. 3¾" × 2".

figure 4.16 Floral Brooch. Eisenberg Original Marked Eisenberg and Sterling, mid-1940s. The large center clear rhinestone is surrounded by bezel set clears layered over open-work leaves that curl and are lined with clear rhinestones. Dimensional. 1¾" × 2".

figure 4.17

figure 4.18

figure 4.19

figure 4.17 Floral Fur Clip. Marked Eisenberg Original and Sterling, mid-1940s. Three-dimensional flowered piece with clear marquis rhinestones and clear pavé sets. 2½" × 2".

figure 4.18 Dimensional floral fur clip marked Eisenberg Original and Sterling, mid-1940s. Large, clear center rhinestone surrounded by intricate and dimensional layers of bezel set rhinestones with leaf motif. 2½" × 2⅛".

figure 4.19 Source unknown, c. 1948.

figure 4.20 *Vogue*, September 1, 1947.

figure 4.21

figure 4.22

figure 4.21 Demi-Parure of Earrings and Brooches. Brooches Marked Script E and Sterling. Clip earrings marked Block E and Sterling, c. 1945. Sets mirror each other with prong, bezel, and pavé set clears forming abstract floral designs. Brooches 1½" × 1¼". Earrings 1¼" × ¾".

figure 4.22 Abstract Floral Dress Clip. Marked Eisenberg Original Sterling, c. mid-1940s. Stems arching on top with five large emerald-cut clear stones and four bezel-set rhinestones. Bottom of stems bend backward with rows of pavé set stones. 3" × 2¼".

figure 4.23 *Vogue*, September 15, 1944.

Eisenberg Ice,

the famous costume jewelry.
Imported original crystal stones.
Each set in sterling silver
and stamped with the
Eisenberg hallmark of quality.

EISENBERG JEWELRY, INC. • Merchandise Mart • Chicago 54, Illinois

figure 4.24
Vogue, April 1, 1945.

figure 4.25

figure 4.26

figure 4.27

figure 4.25 Clear Fur Clip with Icy Blue Accents. Eisenberg Original, Marked Eisenberg & Sterling. Advertised in 1945. Large, open-backed clear stones arc down while bands of clear pavé set rounds shoot from two large center stones of the palest blue. 3¼" × 2¼".

figure 4.26 Icy Blue Bouquet Brooch. Marked Eisenberg Original & Sterling. Advertised in 1945. The piece is layered with each row building on the previous row. Clear bezel set stones encircle each blue flower. 3½" × 3".

figure 4.27 Icy Blue Fur Clip. Marked Eisenberg Original & Sterling, c. 1945. In *Jewels of Fantasy. Costume Jewelry of the 20th Century* showcases this as a stylized feather. Heavy sterling design with pale blue marquis crystals. Accents of clear bezel and pavé set rhinestones. 3¾" × 2½".

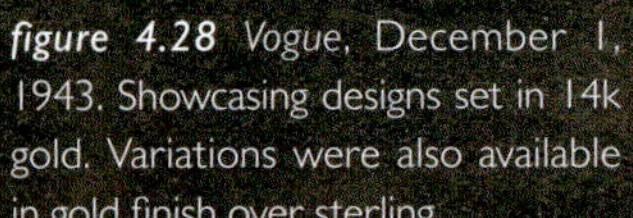

figure 4.28 Vogue, December 1, 1943. Showcasing designs set in 14k gold. Variations were also available in gold finish over sterling.

figure 4.29

figure 4.30

figure 4.31

figure 4.32

figure 4.33

figure 4.29 Rare 14k bow pin #21. Marked Eisenberg Original and Sterling. All these vermeil bows were numbered. A direct copy of the 14k styling also features the large emerald-cut genuine Brazilian topaz quartz center stone. 2⅞" × 2⅓".

figure 4.30 Topaz Earrings. Marked Script E and Sterling, c. 1943. The Eisenberg ad lists, but does not show, these less expensive vermeil over sterling pieces. These actually have more elaborate bow detailing than their 14k cousins. All these pieces featured "genuine Brazilian topaz quartz." Screw back. 1" × 1".

figure 4.31 Topaz and Gold Fur Clip. Eisenberg Original Marked Eisenberg and Sterling, mid-1940s. Gold vermeil ribbons lined with clears curl out from a large center emerald-cut topaz stone. Bezel set clears run along the top. 2¼" × 2".

figure 4.32 Blue and Gold Fur Clip. Eisenberg Original Marked Eisenberg and Sterling, mid-1940s. Same as previous piece, but with the blue emerald-cut center stone.

figure 4.33 Golden Bow Brooch. Marked Eisenberg Original and Sterling, mid-1940s. Gold wash. Massive metal loops hang above two massive citrine stones. Center of ribbon is a band of pavé set clears that also accent one of the metal curling ribbon tails. 2⅜" × 2¾".

figure 4.34

figure 4.35

figure 4.36

figure 4.34 Stunning Fur Clip. Marked Eisenberg Original and Sterling, mid-1940s. Woven lines of pavé set clears weave loops around the faceted clear center stone. A pavé lined stylish bale helps to hold the center stone in place. 2⅝" × 2¼".

figure 4.35 Stylized Bouquet with Bow Fur Clip. Eisenberg Original Marked Eisenberg and Sterling, mid-1940s. Sterling stems are topped with clear round and marquis blooms. Ribbon work is lined in clear bezel and pavé set stones. A large clear oval anchors the ribbon at the bottom. 3" × 2½".

figure 4.36 Abstract Fur Clip. Eisenberg Original Marked Eisenberg and Sterling, mid-1940s. Highly stylized with a bottom layer of strands that arch backward, some set with clears. The top strands fold over and are tipped with rectangular clears. Bezel set clears rest just below them. 3" × 2¼".

figure 4.37 Inverted Floral Bouquet Fur Clip. Eisenberg Original Marked Eisenberg and Sterling, mid-1940s. Bright oval and round clears form both small and large blooms dangling from sterling stems. Bouquet is wrapped with clear pavé set lines imitating ribbon detailing. 3½" × 2¼".

figure 4.38 Snowflake Brooch. Marked Script E and Sterling, mid-1940s. Icy clear stones form this unique three-dimensional design. The large center round has spokes done with ovals that are tipped with navettes. Ribbon loops of pavé and bezel set stones drape backward. 3" diameter.

figure 4.37

figure 4.38

figure 4.39 Source unknown, c. 1945.

figure 4.40 Source unknown, c. 1945.

figure 4.41

figure 4.42

figure 4.43

figure 4.41 Ruby and Turquoise Bracelet. Marked Sterling, c. 1945. Though it does not bear the Eisenberg signature, this was found with a matching marked fur clip and is identical to the bracelet in the advertisement. Gold wash sterling with mirrored tapered half-moons of red glass that form links separated by faux turquoise beads. 7¾" × ¾".

figure 4.42 Dimensional Fur Clip. Eisenberg Original Marked Eisenberg & Sterling, c. 1945. Gold wash over sterling with large center red cabochon surrounded by tiny clears. Unique bottle-shaped red glass beads lead out to concave petals housing faux turquoise beads. Layered with raised center stone. 2⅜" diameter.

figure 4.43 Poinsettia Brooch. Marked Eisenberg Original & Sterling, advertised Christmas 1944. This gold vermeil brooch uses classic Eisenberg favorites of ruby red and turquoise, here with faux turquoise beads and large red cabochons. 3½" × 2½".

figure 4.44

figure 4.44 Stylized Floral Fur Clip. Eisenberg Original Marked Eisenberg & Sterling, c. 1945. Unique red glass beads lead out from a large center red cabochon surrounded by tiny clears. Concave petals hold faux turquoise beads. Center stone is elevated on top of the many layers. 2½" diameter.

Today, the figural women are Kamke's rarest and the most sought-after by collectors. The design, construction, use of gold wash or plating, and enameling are outstanding. Fish, in real and abstract forms, were her particular favorite. The fantastic mermaid brooch is a complicated design and highly collectible. A series of animals has exquisite detail. Eisenberg's "fighting cocks" were introduced after Cartier had made a smililar pair using real stones.

figure 4.45 Ballerina Brooch, Eisenberg Original Marked Eisenberg and Sterling, mid-1940s. Gold vermeil. Emerald rhinestones center the flowers of her skirt and headdress with clear stones acting as petals and shoulder decorations. Enameling decorates her body, shoes, face, and nails. 3¼" × 2½".

figure 4.46

figure 4.47

figure 4.48

figure 4.49

figure 4.46 Can-Can Dancer Brooch. Eisenberg Original Marked Eisenberg and Sterling, advertised March 1946. Gold vermeil. Clear rhinestones outline her skirt and headdress and dot her shoes. Red enameling highlights her costume and face. Two pieces hinged together for dimension. 3½" × 2".

figure 4.47 Lady with Scarf Brooch, a.k.a. Dancer and Ballerina. Eisenberg Original Marked Eisenberg and Sterling, mid-1940s. Gold vermeil. Costume accents are clear and emerald-green stones and black and green enameling touches. 3½" × 2".

figure 4.48 Cleaning Woman with Bucket Fur Clip. Marked Eisenberg Original and Sterling, mid-1940s. This version has the bucket and brush. Gold vermeil. Carved details for her clothing and face are accented with multiple colors of enamel. Clear rhinestones band her bucket, shoulders, and waist. 2⅞" × 1⅞".

figure 4.49 Cleaning Woman with Broom Fur Clip. Marked Eisenberg Original and Sterling, mid-1940s. Gold vermeil. Woman carrying broom over her shoulder. Green, black, and red enameling accents on dress, apron, and shoes. Scattered rhinestones on band on hat. 3" × 1⅞".

figure 4.50

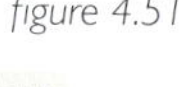

figure 4.51

figure 4.52

figure 4.53

figure 4.50 Figural Fish Brooch. Marked Eisenberg Original, c. 1940. Gold plated. Large aqua faceted stones form the body and tail fins with a small aqua stone for the eye. Black enameling highlights the gaping mouth, which has a tiny line of clear stones set above it. 2¾" × 3".

figure 4.51 Fish Brooch. Marked Eisenberg Original, 1942. Gold plate over pot metal body with the top and tail fins made of ruby marquis-cut stones, each outlined with clear bezel sets. Clears also run along the neck and form the eye. 2¾" × 2⅓".

figure 4.52 Fish Brooch. Marked Eisenberg Original and Sterling, mid-1940s. Gold vermeil. Detail abounds from the faux pearls "floating" in rows along the body to the clear rhinestone-accented fins. Touches of enamel add glamour to the face along with clear rhinestone lips. 2.5" long. *Courtesy of Morning Glory Antiques & Jewelry. www.MorningGloryAntiques.com.*

figure 4.53 Oceanic Demi-Parure Fur Clip Marked Eisenberg Original and Sterling, Screw Back Earrings Marked E and Sterling, mid 1940s. Gold vermeil. Seashell designs are centered with aqua stones and surrounded by patterned scallop fans tipped with clear pavé sets. Fur clip 2¾" × 2½". Earrings 1⅛" × 1".

figure 4.54

figure 4.54 Flying Fish Brooch. Marked Eisenberg Original and Sterling, mid-1940s. Gold vermeil. Detailed body of layered scales accented with ruby rhinestones. Ruby stones also accent the tips of the open side fins. Clear pavé set stones enhance the fins. Hints of black enameling. 3¼" × 2½".

figure 4.55

figure 4.56

figure 4.57

figure 4.58

figure 4.55 Abstract Dolphins Fur Clip. Marked Eisenberg Original and Sterling, mid-1940s. Gold vermeil. Bottom blue oval rhinestone represents the water with golden dolphins arching upward, each accented with clear pavé sets and capped with three blue round stones. 2¼" × 2¼".

figure 4.56 Nautilus Brooch. Marked Eisenberg Original and Sterling, mid-1940s. Fourteen emerald-cut deep amethyst rhinestones swirl in a pattern evoking the nautilus shell. Pavé set clears outline the inner design and bezel set clears accent the outside. 2⅝" × 3¼".

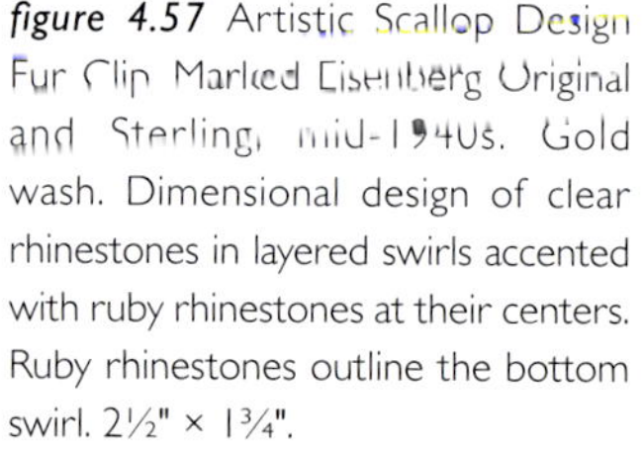

figure 4.57 Artistic Scallop Design Fur Clip. Marked Eisenberg Original and Sterling, mid-1940s. Gold wash. Dimensional design of clear rhinestones in layered swirls accented with ruby rhinestones at their centers. Ruby rhinestones outline the bottom swirl. 2½" × 1¾".

figure 4.58 Marine Inspired Fur Clip. Marked Eisenberg Original and Sterling, mid-1940s. Paisley inspired swirls done with layered teardrop clears. Top arches out and folds backwards. Pavé set clears outline the curves. 1½" × 1½".

figure 4.59 Abstract Snail Fur Clip. Marked Eisenberg Original and Sterling, mid-1940s. Gold wash over sterling. Clear rhinestones cover the top arch and outline the curlicue swirl. Pink and amethyst marquis-cut rhinestones fan out around the bottom. 1½" × 1¼". *From the Collection of Joanna van Ritbergen.*

figure 4.60

figure 4.61

figure 4.62

figure 4.63

figure 4.60 Mermaid Brooch. Marked Eisenberg Original & Sterling, advertised in *Vogue*, c. 1946. Her torso has a faceted, open-backed aquamarine stone and she holds streaming strands of aquamarine cut crystals. Gold vermeil with accents of small clear rounds and red enamel lipstick and nail polish. This mermaid bears a remarkable resemblance to Verdura's Naiad Clip done with real pearls and diamonds. Eisenberg's mermaid is one of the most highly sought after pieces for collectors. 3¼" × 2¾".

figure 4.61 Figural Prancing Zebra Brooch. Marked Eisenberg Original and Sterling, mid-1940s. Carved body is beautifully accented with green enameling. Black enameling accents on tail, hooves, and face. Interesting eye. Body is underlined by small clear rhinestones. 2" × 3½".

figure 4.62 Bull Fur Clip. Eisenberg Original Marked Eisenberg and Sterling, mid-1940s. Gold vermeil. Detailed with dimensional carved head and twisting horns accented with clear rhinestones. Ears are emerald-green teardrop stones. A link chain hangs about the neck holding an emerald cowbell rhinestone. 2" × 3¾".

figure 4.63 Prancing Horse Brooch. Marked Eisenberg Original, late 1930s. Heavy gold plating. Incised stars decorate the body and are centered with a clear rhinestone. Carved mane and tail are accented with black enameling, as is the face. Red enamel hooves spotlight the horse's gait. 2" × 2¾".

figure 4.64

figure 4.65

figure 4.66

figure 4.67

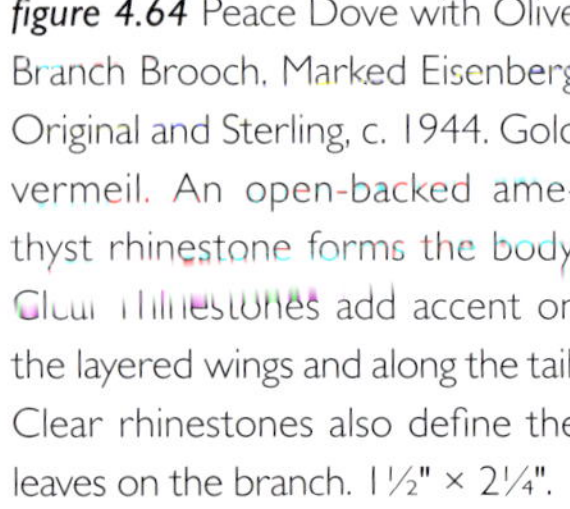

figure 4.64 Peace Dove with Olive Branch Brooch. Marked Eisenberg Original and Sterling, c. 1944. Gold vermeil. An open-backed amethyst rhinestone forms the body. Clear rhinestones add accent on the layered wings and along the tail. Clear rhinestones also define the leaves on the branch. 1½" × 2¼".

figure 4.65 Butterfly Brooch. Marked Eisenberg Original and Sterling, mid-1940s. Body is a faceted topaz stone with two tiny topaz stones dotting the antennae. Giant sweeping lacy wings are outlined in tiny clears and tiny clears form the head. 2¾" × 2¾".

figure 4.66 Fighting Cocks. Marked Eisenberg Original & Sterling, c. 1945. Heavy gold wash over sterling. Colored rhinestone eyes with clear pavé rhinestones along the feathers. Have been seen with and without enameling. Inspired by a design by Cartier. 2½" × 1¾".

figure 4.67 Bird on a Branch Brooch. Marked Eisenberg Original, Sterling, c. 1943–1944. Gold wash sterling. Enameling on stems and feathers, large center emerald-green stone on bird, pavé set rhinestones on feathers and leaves. 1¼" × 2¼".

Not every piece of sterling jewelry Eisenberg marketed in the Original years came from F&K. With so much sterling coming from Mexico, Eisenberg was exposed to Mexican artists and purchased some of their designs, including pieces made of faux jade stones that were dyed onyx or calcite.

figure 4.68

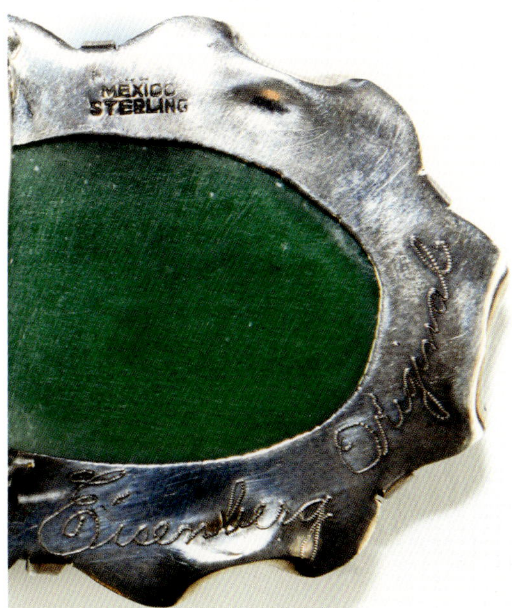

figure 4.69

figure 4.70

figure 4.71

figure 4.68 Mexican Face Brooch. Signed Eisenberg Original in hand script and marked Sterling, mid-1940s. Large faux jade face prong set in sterling frame. Bears the Aztec feel of many of these pieces. 2½" × 2".

figure 4.69 Eisenberg Original in handwritten script bearing the mark Sterling Mexico

figure 4.70 Large Mexican Faux Jade Fish Brooch. Signed Eisenberg Original in hand script and silver, mid-1940s. Dimensional detailing in sterling defines the face and fins in this fun design with the huge domed faux jade cabochon. 2⅝" × 2¾"× 3¼" overall. *From the Collection of Laura Sutton.*

figure 4.71 Eisenberg Original in handwritten script bearing the mark Made in Mexico Sterling.

Eisenberg was not the only company heading "south of the border" for sterling, and you will often see similar pieces for sale from its competitors. These pieces come from the same time period and the same artists; however, the Eisenberg pieces were always marked in the Eisenberg Original handwritten script; there are two variations of silver markings.

figure 4.72

figure 4.73

figure 4.74

figure 4.75

figure 4.72 Mexican Cupid's Heart Faux Jade Brooch. Signed Eisenberg Original in hand script and stamped "Sterling," mid-1940s. The faux jade stone is carved into a heart and framed in sterling. This is a rare design and is quite fun with the arrows piercing the piece. Very large at 4⅝" × 2".

figure 4.73 Mexican Faux Jade Pendant. Marked Eisenberg Original and Sterling, mid-1940s. The faux jade stone has beautiful color variations and is cut in a subtle curving wave design. 2¾" × 1¾".

figure 4.74 Mexican Faux Jade Floral Brooch. Marked Eisenberg Original and Sterling, mid-1940s. Cut and twisted to appear like petals in bloom. Quite a bit of depth is achieved with the carving. 2¼" × 2¼".

figure 4.75 Pair of Faux Jade Mexican Brooches. Marked Eisenberg Original and Sterling, mid-1940s. This matched set of carved figural brooches are designed to resemble ancient Aztec carvings. 1¾" × 1½".

Did You Know
They Made Those?
Eisenberg's Unexpected Treasures

Did You Know They Made Those?

As Eisenberg moved into the 1940s, its jewelry line was growing rapidly, its clothing line was doing well, and the perfume division was firmly established. The Eisenbergs decided to find out what else might be successful.

Fashion Accessories

figure 5.1

The company's colorful, shawl-sized scarves were first advertised in the mid-1940s, and the story behind them is fascinating. It begins with a French count born in 1900, named Rene Bouet-Willaumez, who would become one of *Vogue's* most dramatic artists. He started work with *Vogue* in 1929, but it was in the 1940s that *Vogue* particularly favored him. Tasked with capturing the creations of the most recognized names in fashion, his drawings have become highly collectible. Count Rene's "RBW" signature can be found on some of the dreamiest fashion illustrations of the time. In the 1950s, photography began replacing illustrations, and Rene faded from sight. After his death in 1979, his widow opened their home to guests and spoke about her husband's career.

figure 5.1 Flowers In Vase Scarf. Labeled Eisenberg Original. Signed RBW, c. 1940s. Bright blue border frames a classical vase on a polka dot tablecloth. Bursting above it is an abstract bouquet of many floral varieties boldly accented with color. An original painting, the shadows are highlighted. 39" × 36".

figure 5.2 *Vogue*, c. 1938. Rene Bouet-Willaumez fashion for Bergdorf Goodman. *From the Collection of Laura Sutton.*

In 1941, at the height of his success with both American and European *Vogue*, Rene did a unique project with Saks Fifth Avenue.[1] Partnering with an engraving company and a printing company, he saw his sketches transferred with complete accuracy to white silk canvases. Presented as either wall or wearable art, and in a wide variety of subject matter, these creations were backed by the Combier Chauvin Silk Corporation. Their debut at Saks Fifth Avenue unfolded with all the prestige of a museum exhibit opening. The original silk creations were sold only at Saks Fifth Avenue and took pride of place in their coveted windows.

A few years later, Combier Chauvin partnered with Eisenberg & Sons to create a rayon version of the scarves. Bearing the moniker Eisenberg Original and Eisenberg Originals, these pieces contain the RBW initials.

OPPOSITE

figure 5.3 *Vogue*, c. 1948. Rene Bouet-Willaumez original print showcasing a day at the races.

figure 5.3

figure 5.4 Source unknown, c. 1943. Rene Bouet-Willaumez original pen and ink fashion designs. *From the Collection of Laura Sutton.*

The long view

LONG or short evening dress? There's no controversy. Each has its place. At an Officers' dance, benefit gala, dinner-party where transportation is no problem—long ones belong. All the High Couture include them in their new Collections.

FIRST: Long and full and filmy is this dress that Sophie designed of unrationed black net with printed panels (by Willaumez) appliquéd with yellow roses. Salon Moderne, Saks-Fifth Ave.

SECOND: Slim and semi-covered up is this blue rayon crêpe sheath, its hem-line shorter in front, its sole decoration beaded pink and yellow satin sash ends. Hattie Carnegie Original

THIRD: Slim and totally covered up is this evening suit of white rayon crêpe, its skirt a mere tube, its jacket embroidered with little fans of beads, a flame scarf. Henri Bendel Original

figure 5.5 Source unknown, c. 1943. Rene Bouet-Willaumez original pen and ink fashion designs. *From the Collection of Laura Sutton.*

The original review of the showing at Saks Fifth Avenue references hundreds of silk squares adorning the walls, but contains no mention of exactly how many variations were sold through Saks Fifth Avenue. We were also unable to find an exact count of how many of the designs Eisenberg used, but it was likely at least a dozen. We have six in our collections, and one is shown in an advertisement. Another ad from 1946 shows four designs, three of which are different from ours. Each design was offered in multiple colors and styles.

Beginning in 1945, Eisenberg started to mention the scarves in its advertised product lists, and they were given their own category. Despite the attention the company gave them, there is no indication that the scarves were offered for more than a few years. They rarely come on the market now, and we were unable to find any images of Count Bouet-Willaumez's original silk pieces, or any reference to a recent sale. This makes both the silk and rayon versions worth seeking out.

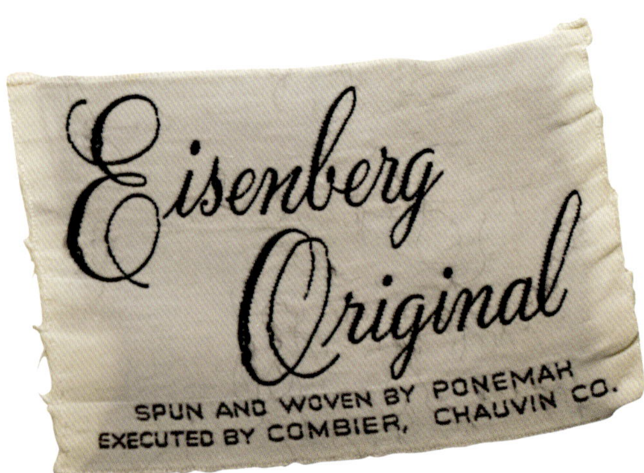

figure 5.6

figure 5.7

figure 5.6 Scarf label indicating Eisenberg Original with maker Combier, Chauvin; spun and woven by Ponemah.

figure 5.7 Same as previous label with the exception of using the Originals designation.

figure 5.8

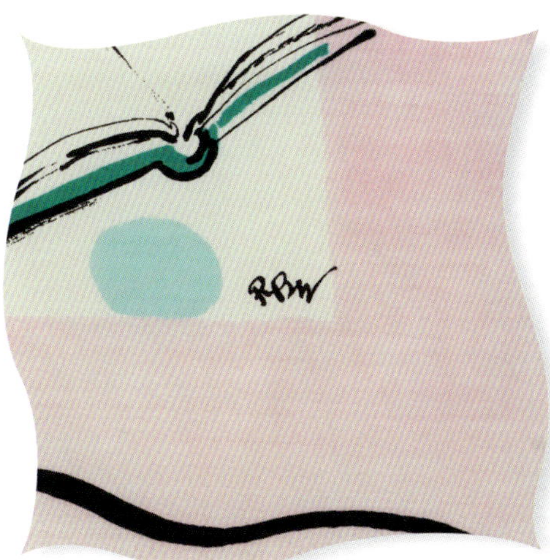

figure 5.9

figure 5.10

figure 5.8 Hyacinth Scarf. Labeled Eisenberg Original. Signed RBW, mid-1940s. Table display of a gift-wrapped pot of colored hyacinths with large bow. An open book shares the table and patterned curtains drape behind. Colors of pinks, green, aqua, and cream with black accents. 38" × 36".

figure 5.9 Same scarf as above highlighting RBW initials in lower right corner.

figure 5.10 Celebration Scarf. Labeled Eisenberg Original. Signed RBW, mid-1940s. A striking black and orange detailed border frames three costumed figures. Not quite Harlequins or Jesters, so perhaps they are enjoying Carnival? Done with green, orange, pink, cream, and Rene's signature black strokes. 38" × 36".

figure 5.11

figure 5.12

figure 5.13

figure 5.11 Colorful Floral Scarf. Labeled Eisenberg Original. Signed RBW, c. 1940s. All we can think of when we see this piece is "Mirror mirror on the wall." Center piece is an elaborately framed mirror with floral and scrollwork detailing in purple, blue, and black. Surrounding it is an entire garden of blooms. 37" × 34".

figure 5.12 Shakespeare Themed Scarf. Labeled Eisenberg Original. Signed RBW, c. 1940s. There is no official name for this piece, but it does remind one of a classic playwright's desk with the feather quill, the inkwell, and the many written pages in front of a wall of books. 38" × 38".

figure 5.13 Yellow Rose Scarf. Labeled Eisenberg Originals. Signed RBW, c. 1940s. The center is a multi-hued American beauty rose. Surrounding it are birds, bugs, and butterflies with a hand-drawn feel and with accents of bold color. 38" square. *From the Collection of Laura Sutton.*

figure 5.14 Source unknown, c. 1945. Colossal scarfs. Magnificent in color and size, spun and woven by Ponemah and executed by Combier Chauvin.

Did You Know They Made Those?

Eisenberg also manufactured handbags. These were most likely done in the mid- to late-1940s, based on their styling and materials. A rare mention of the handbags appeared in *Women's Wear Daily* on January 27, 1958, in an announcement that listed the handbags as one of the expansions the company had embraced through the years. There is no record of advertising. Handbags discovered on the market have been black and had different materials, shapes, and styles, but all were decorated with clear rhinestone and marked Eisenberg Original.

figure 5.15

figure 5.16

figure 5.17

figure 5.18

figure 5.15 Black Suede Handbag. Labeled Eisenberg Originals, c. 1950. Black suede with decorative suede foldover flaps held by two stunning clear rhinestone buttons. Gold hardware with push button clasp. Concealable strap. 9¼" × 8¼".

figure 5.16 Pair of rhinestone buttons shown from previous handbag. 1¼" diameter.

figure 5.17 Velvet Handbag. Labeled Eisenberg Originals, c. 1950. Clutch design with wide arching front flap. Decorated with a 2" domed clear rhinestone adornment. Lined in black satin. Snap closure. 5½" × 12".

figure 5.18 Close-up of rhinestone adornment.

figure 5.19

figure 5.20

figure 5.21

figure 5.22

figure 5.19 Black Brocade Handbag. Labeled Eisenberg Originals, c. 1950. Handbag is a clutch in a beautifully patterned black brocade with clear, round rhinestones accented with Eisenberg's half-moons set with pavé clear rhinestones. Original accessories include change purse and mirror in brocade. 7½" × 14".

figure 5.20 Close-up of the rhinestone.

figure 5.21 Original handbag accessories in matching brocade.

figure 5.22 Interior of brocade handbag showing Eisenberg Originals label and pockets.

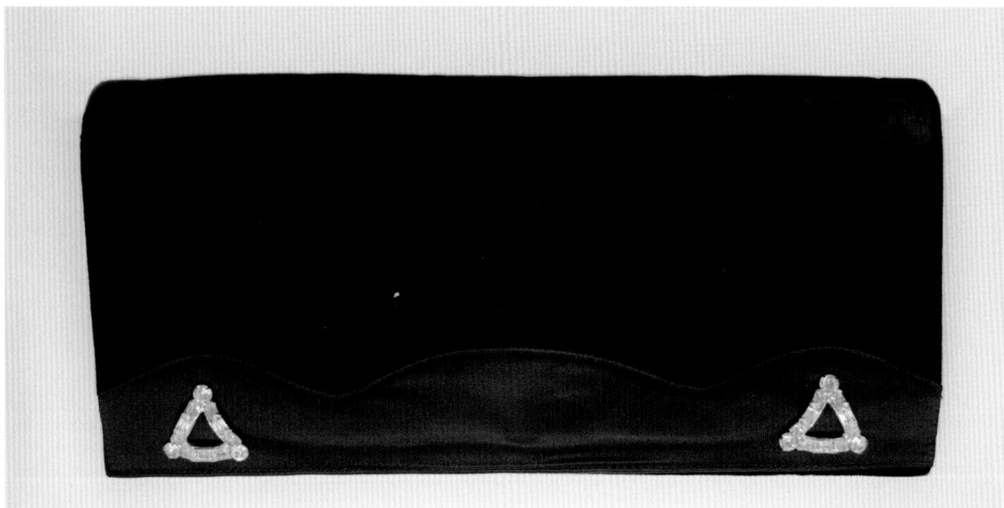

figure 5.23

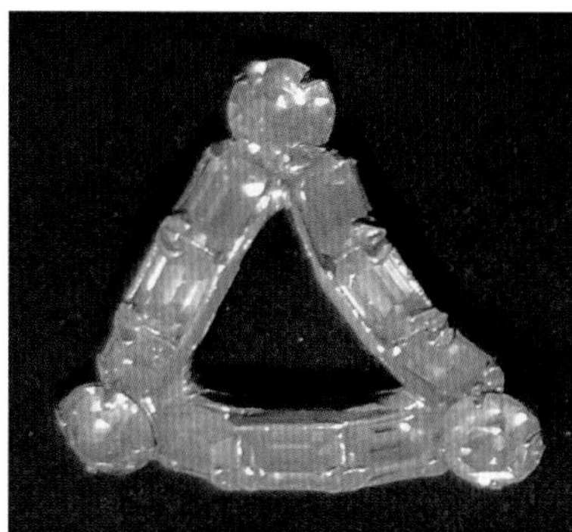

figure 5.24

figure 5.23 Black Velvet Handbag. Labeled Eisenberg Originals, c. 1950. Handbag is a clutch with the bottom half of the fold-over front flap decorated with a black satin band and two clear rhinestone triangles of emerald and round cuts. 6" × 12". *From the Collection of Laura Sutton.*

figure 5.24 Close-up of triangular adornment for previous clutch.

Belts and buckles are another extremely rare category of Eisenberg creations. Kamke remembers designing them through the years, yet few have been seen on the market. Where have they all gone?

OPPOSITE
figure 5.25 *Vogue*, August 15, 1937. The car in this ad is from a long-gone era and reminds us of just how vintage these pieces are. Only one belt is specifically mentioned as carved aluminum, though both are likely metal based on their designs.

Eisenberg & Sons
Original
For Football Saturdays, this suit of a special Forstmann tweed, exclusive with Eisenberg. For afternoon dancing, this dress of sheer black wool with a carved aluminum belt. Identified by the Eisenberg label and shown in fine stores throughout the country. Write us for the name of the store in your city.
EISENBERG & SONS • DRESSMAKERS • 847 JACKSON BOULEVARD, CHICAGO
HATS, BAGS AND SHOES BY I. MILLER • PHOTOGRAPH BY ARTHUR O'NEILL

figure 5.25

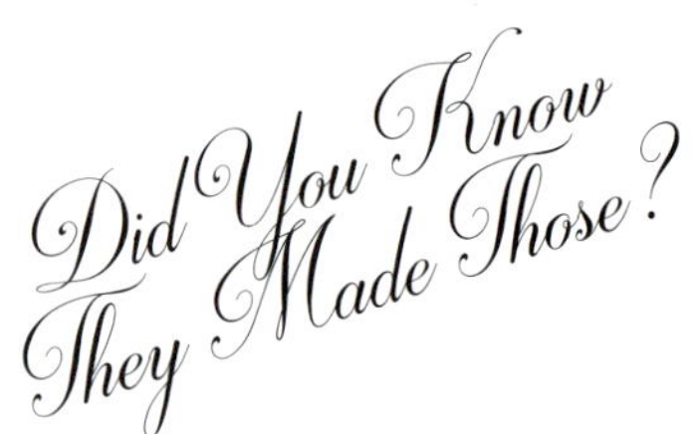

figure 5.26

figure 5.27

figure 5.28

figure 5.29

figure 5.26 Faux Turquoise Belt. Marked Eisenberg Original, late 1930s. Center decoration of large faux turquoise stones in various shapes and sizes accented with a variety of clear bezel sets. Silver pot metal with floral designs. Links are etched with scrollwork and end at bars with faux turquoise beads. Belt length 12½".

figure 5.27 Source unknown, late 1940. This delightful ad features a feminine ruffled dress belted with a double loop snakeskin belt. Note the striking contrast between feminine detailing and a more masculine finishing touch.

figure 5.28 Rear view showing the Eisenberg Original mark.

figure 5.29 Triple Row Rhinestone Belt. Marked Block E, c. 1950s. Rhodium base for the three strands of clear rhinestones accented by large open metal links. 36" × ⅓" with ¾" ring accents.

Vanity Accessories

Immediately after Eisenberg Jewelry was formed, the company launched a secondary line of vanity accessories, beginning with compacts. They were metal, gold tone, encrusted with jewels, and marked Eisenberg Original on the lid or the bottom.

figure 5.30

figure 5.31

figure 5.32

figure 5.33

figure 5.30 Mirrored Compact. Marked Eisenberg Original on powder lid, c. 1940s. Unusual exterior beveled mirror edged in small multi-color prong set rounds. Interior also has a mirror and the powder compartment as shown in the next image. Has original box. 3¼" diameter.

figure 5.31 Interior view.

figure 5.32 Colorful Compact. Marked Eisenberg Original on powder lid and puff, c. 1940s. The wide circular design has an inner band of gold triangles holding bezel set clears, a row of multi-color round stones, and a row of multi-color marquis stones interspersed with bezel set clears. 3½" diameter.

figure 5.33 Round Compact with Elaborate Rhinestone Bow. Marked Eisenberg Original on powder lid, c. 1940s. Silver pot metal ribbon bow has scalloped edges and is done with clear rhinestones that are both bezel and pavé set. 3¼" diameter.

figure 5.34 *An early advertisement showcased the square compact. Source unknown.*

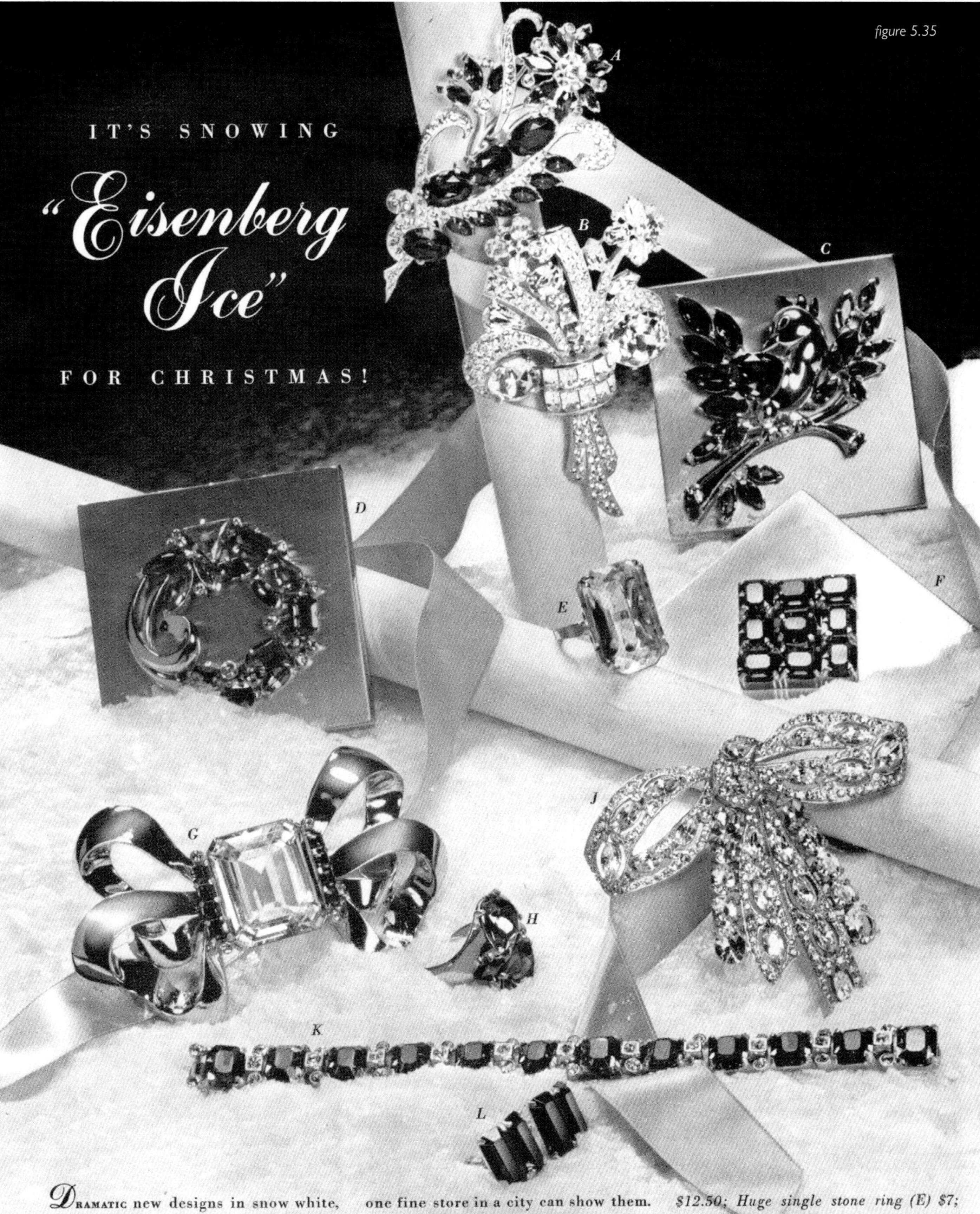

Dramatic new designs in snow white, ruby red and other jewel colors. Eisenberg compacts, too, with fabulous ornaments. Gifts that are *so* special because these large-cut stones are *so* rare, because only one fine store in a city can show them. APPROXIMATE PRICES *(subject to Federal Excise Tax): Spray clip (A) $15; Cluster clip (B) $15.50; Compact with bird ornament (C) $16.50; Compact with multi-colored stones (D) $12.50; Huge single stone ring (E) $7; Compact with square ornament (F) $10; Gold bow-knot with white stone center (G) $12.50; Two-stone ring (H) $8; Snow white bow-knot (J) $21.50; Bracelet (K) $13.50; Earrings (L) $5.*

Merchandise Mart **Eisenberg Jewelry, Inc.** Chicago

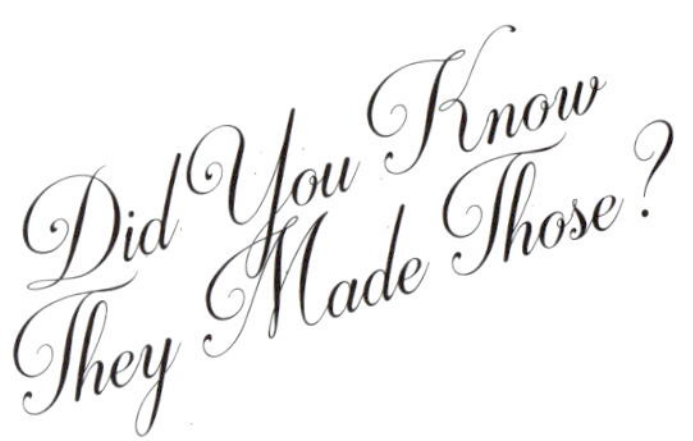

An ad from 1941 is clearly intended for holiday shopping (previous page). The compact on the left is decorated with a multi-color wreath; the compact laying down features a multi-stone solid-color decorative square (this design appeared on a bracelet from the same year), and the one on the right showcases a bird on a branch.

The compacts apparently disappeared for a time in the mid-1940s, because an ad in *Vogue* on February 1, 1947, stated that "Compacts from Eisenberg are again available."[2] We know the company dabbled in cigarette cases, too, but it is likely that fewer were made.

figure 5.36

figure 5.37

figure 5.38

PREVIOUS PAGE
figure 5.35 *Harpers Bazaar*, c. 1941. Advertisement highlights square compact.

figure 5.36 Source unknown, c. 1947.

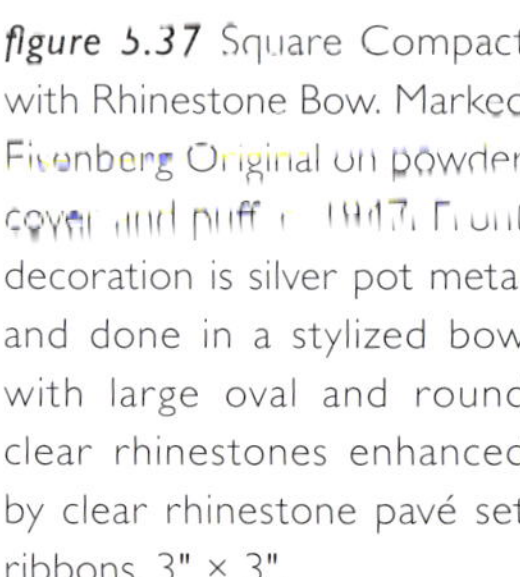

figure 5.37 Square Compact with Rhinestone Bow. Marked Eisenberg Original on powder cover and puff, c. 1947. Front decoration is silver pot metal and done in a stylized bow with large oval and round clear rhinestones enhanced by clear rhinestone pavé set ribbons. 3" × 3".

figure 5.38 Eisenberg Original mark on powder compartment lid.

figure 5.39

figure 5.40

figure 5.41

The perfume division cross-pollinated the handbag designs with stylish accessories. Kamke remembered there were at least four different handbag accessories to hold the company's rhinestone bottles.[3] We have only seen two.

figure 5.42

figure 5.39 Square Compact with Patriotic-Colored Stones. Marked Eisenberg Original on compact cover and puff, c. 1943. Gold pot metal. Red, white, and blue ½" prong and bezel set stones in triangular pattern. 3" × 3".

figure 5.40 Cigarette Case with Rhinestone Bow. Marked Eisenberg Original on bottom of case. The original interior cigarette tray is still present. A silver pot metal dimensional ribbon bow done with clear rhinestones decorates the bottom right corner of the case. Found in original box with flannel protective cover. 3" × 5½".

figure 5.41 One of the variations of the figural lady is shown here on the interior label of the cigarette case.

figure 5.42 Purse Perfume Flacon. Marked Eisenberg Original, c. 1940s. This golden bottle is tipped with three clear crystal stones in oval, marquis, and square cuts. Found in original satin pouch. 2⅞" × ½".

figure 5.43

figure 5.44

A lipstick mirror in the shape of lips with an Eisenberg Originals pouch would seem to date to the 1940s. However, the design probably comes from the 1960s or later due to its Eisenberg Ice label and patent number. It is hard to imagine that Eisenberg would have made pouches just for these mirrors, yet so many are still in their sleeve that it appears they were sold this way. The whimsical design makes it a favorite among collectors.

figure 5.45

figure 5.43 Jeweled Perfume Bottle. Marked Eisenberg and Stirring, c. 1940s. Contains twenty-three multi-colored prong set round rhinestones. 2¼" × 1".

figure 5.44 A Day to Night Delight. Marked "Startling by Eisenberg" and "Excitement by Eisenberg" on opposite ends, c. 1940s. This double fragrance purse bottle has glass ends held by the center gold portion. With original carrying pouch. 3⅛" × ⅝".

figure 5.45 Lipstick Mirror in Shape of Lips, c. 1940s.

Truly Unique Creations

There are a few one-of-a-kind pieces, such as a rare locket, clip pins, and charms. The locket is the only known locket design from Eisenberg, and for decades the collecting community had speculated about its origin. The previous owner had two theories. One was that it was a one-of-a-kind design made for a family member or customer; with much speculation about the identity of the person in the photo that the locket contains. The other theory was that it was a prototype that never went into production.

figure 5.46

figure 5.47

figure 5.48

figure 5.46 Rare Locket Dress Clip. Marked Eisenberg Original. Centered with a square-cut rhinestone. Pavé set clears ring the center stone with large emerald-cut clear rhinestones top and bottom. Bezel set clears add accent. 3¼" × 1 ¾".

figure 5.47 Center Stone Open. The immense 1¼" × 1¼" center stone lifts to reveal your treasured love.

figure 5.48 Lift the dress clip to open the locket.

Did You Know They Made Those?

It seemed like its origins would remain a mystery. Then a couple of years ago, an Eisenberg photo of the locket appeared. The inscription reads: "One of our super-modish dressmakers has designed a stunning [rhinestone is crossed out here] clip for day or night wear which opens to disclose a miniature image of your own true love. Shown above on a cloud pink wool house gown, it is composed of one large and beautifully cut stone which flies opens, set in a frame of rhinestones." It is dated 3-15-40. Because Eisenberg intended to advertise the piece, this is probably not the only one out there, but it is likely that only a few made it to market. A piece this complicated would not have been easy or affordable to manufacture. It is fascinating that the piece is credited to one of Eisenberg's dressmakers. Might it have been Irma Kirby?

figure 5.49

figure 5.50

figure 5.51

figure 5.49 Model wearing rare locket pin. *Photo by Charmante Studio, New York.*

figure 5.50 Back of photo.

figure 5.51 Close-up of postcard back.

The clip-pin was patented by Louis Cartier in 1927. The defining characteristic of a clip-pin is that it presents itself as a piece of jewelry, usually a brooch. However, the piece is made up of separate components bound together by a metal base.

Not many companies made them, and if you research the term you'll find pieces from CORO or Trifari. It was in the 1930s that CORO debuted its "CORO Duette" and Trifari offered its "Clip-Mate," but there were other companies copying the design, including Eisenberg. Because of the dominance of CORO's pieces, a clip pin is often called a "Duette."

figure 5.52

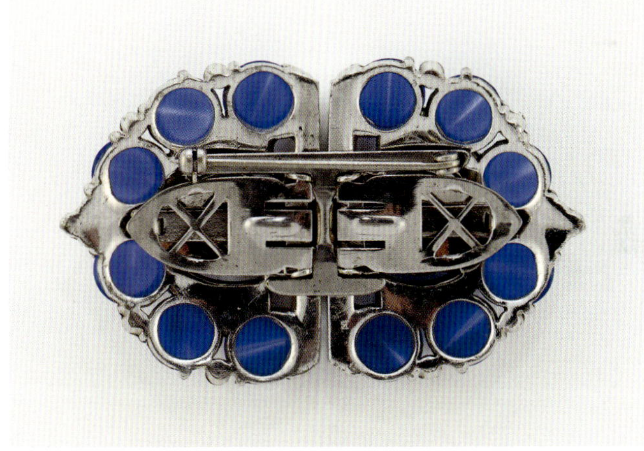

figure 5.53

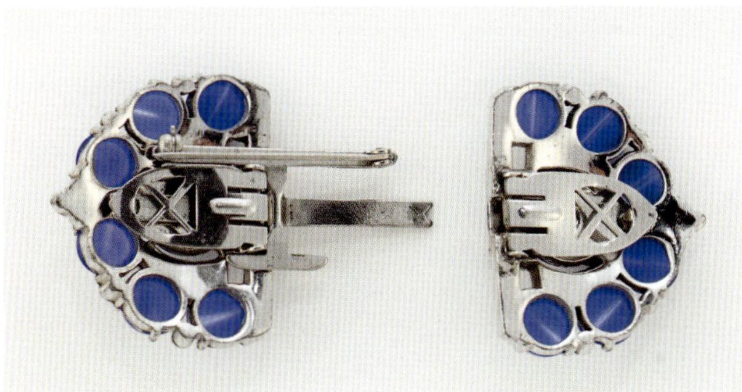

figure 5.54

figure 5.55

figure 5.52 Unique Brooch/Duette. Marked Block E, c. 1950s. Rhodium base. Large blue Lucite moon glow stones are surrounded by pavé and bezel set clears, with baguette clear accents. Piece converts into two separate dress clips. Assembled 1⅝" × 2⅛".

figure 5.53 Back of Duette features two clips held together in a metal frame, forming a brooch.

figure 5.54 Back of Duette showing the separated clips.

figure 5.55 Front of Duette showing the separated clips.

figure 5.56

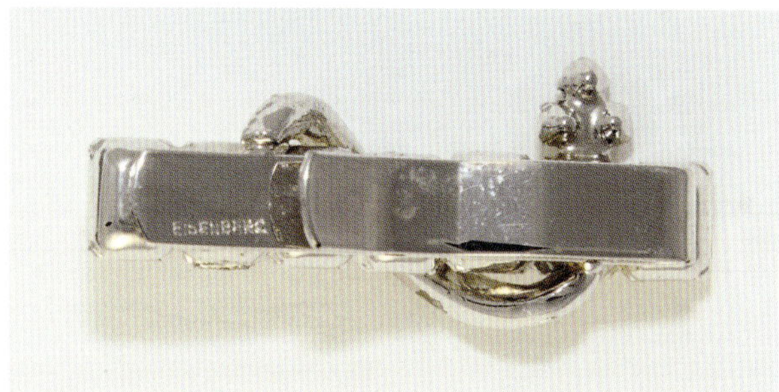

figure 5.57

The design ingenuity of the clip pin shown at left is quite fun, yet the overly complicated elements were expensive to make, and the only other Eisenberg clip-pin we have seen was made entirely of clear rhinestones with an art deco look.

An Eisenberg ad from November 12, 1946, in *Women's Wear Daily* references a category we never dreamed existed—"Grooming Essentials For Men." The closest we've come in our travels is a jeweled tie clip whose styling dates it to the 1950s—later than the ad suggests.

Another unique find was a 12K gold-filled alphabet bracelet charm in its original packaging, probably because the Q would not have been as popular as other letters.

figure 5.58

figure 5.59

figure 5.56 Men's Tie Clip. Marked Block Eisenberg, c. 1950s. Rhodium. Designed with emerald-cut clear rhinestones wrapped with an accent of clear pavé set rhinestones. The only men's accessory we have seen, but we have seen it several times. ¼" × 1¾".

figure 5.57 Back of men's tie clip.

figure 5.58 The original paperwork that was still sealed in the bag with the charm. *From the Collection of Laura Sutton.*

figure 5.59 Alphabet Charm, c. 1950. Tiny letter Q charm for necklace or bracelet. Found sealed in original packaging. ½" × ½". *From the Collection of Laura Sutton.*

Shoe clips were made as early as the 1600s and worn by both men and women. As elaborate fashions faded with the passing centuries, they were largely used for royal or ceremonial occasions.

The 1950s saw a resurgence of the shoe buckle, then referred to as a shoe clip. Many designers offered them as a way to transform the most ordinary shoe into a jeweled accessory. Shoe clips would continue to appear in fashion through the 1980s. They are still available, mostly as bridal accessories.

figure 5.60

figure 5.61

figure 5.60 Unique Shoe Clips. Marked Block E, c. 1950. Gorgeous half circles done with tiny pavé set clears outlined with a graduating line of bezel set clears. Smoky gray round stones decorate half of the exterior fan, with the other half done in clear baguettes. 1⅛" × 1⅞".

figure 5.61 Rear view of shoe clips. Half-circle clips are made of rhodium.

An interesting piece of jewelry appeared in a *Vogue* ad on October 1, 1949. A brooch at first glance, it is actually a flower holder below, and we have seen it in different colors. Tuck flowers into the teeth, close the door, and you were set. The original advertisement suggested using it in hair or to hold a scarf. A small latch keeps the back closed.

figure 5.62

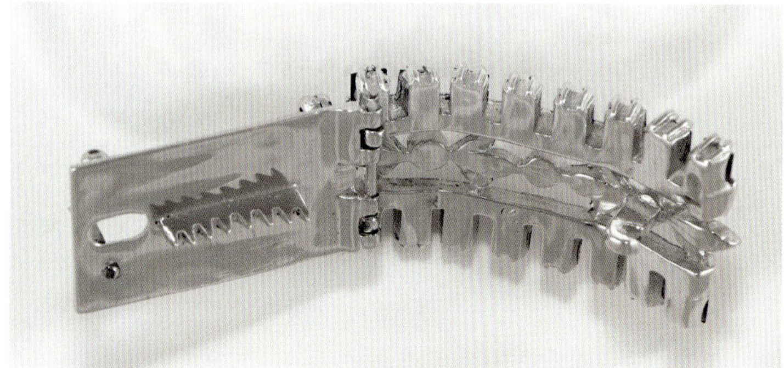

figure 5.63

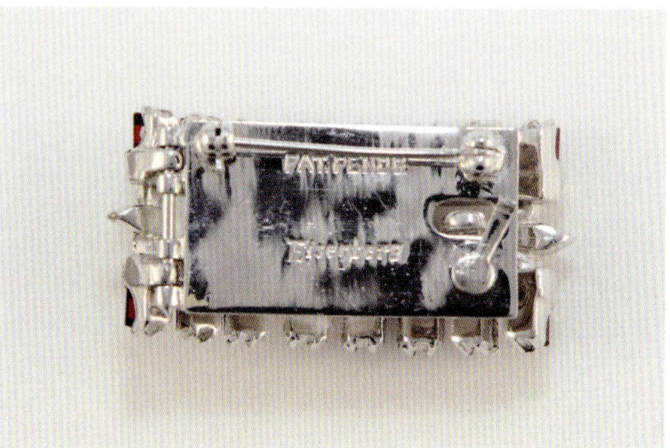

figure 5.64

figure 5.62 Bouquet Brooch. Marked Eisenberg in script and "pat pending," c. 1949. Striking convex brooch. Unique in that it can also hold your floral spray. Rhodium. Red square rhinestones and bezel and pavé set clears. 1¾" × ¾".

figure 5.63 Tuck your flowers into the teeth and close the door, and you are good to go. The original advertisement suggests wearing it in your hair or using it to hold a scarf.

figure 5.64 Advertised in 1949, this image shows the small latch used to keep the secondary back closed. We have seen this piece in three different color combinations.

Lo and behold, an unusual Eisenberg advertisement appeared in *The New Yorker* on September 12, 1970. A throwback to early Eisenberg, the ad was placed by the "Very Saks Fifth Avenue" and featured the "Eisenberg Ice Best of Show... the ultimate dog collar...black velvet and Eisenberg Ice...$25."

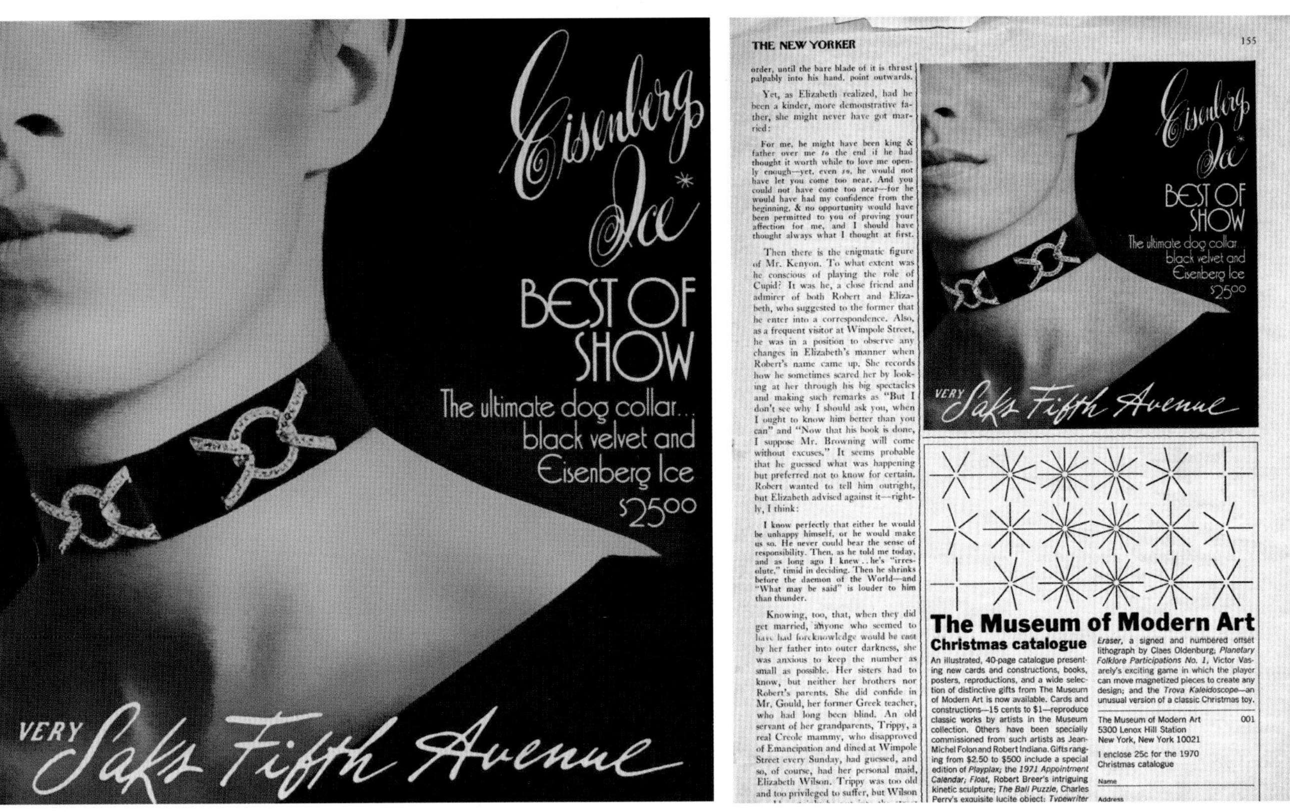

THE NEW YORKER 155

order, until the bare blade of it is thrust palpably into his hand, point outwards.

Yet, as Elizabeth realized, had he been a kinder, more demonstrative father, she might never have got married:

For me, he might have been king & father over me *to* the end if he had thought it worth while to love me openly enough—yet, even *so*, he would not have let you come too near. And you could not have come too near—for he would have had my confidence from the beginning, & no opportunity would have been permitted to you of proving your affection for me, and I should have thought always what I thought at first.

Then there is the enigmatic figure of Mr. Kenyon. To what extent was he conscious of playing the role of Cupid? It was he, a close friend and admirer of both Robert and Elizabeth, who suggested to the former that he enter into a correspondence. Also, as a frequent visitor at Wimpole Street, he was in a position to observe any changes in Elizabeth's manner when Robert's name came up. She records how he sometimes scared her by looking at her through his big spectacles and making such remarks as "But I don't see why I should ask you, when I ought to know him better than you can" and "Now that his book is done, I suppose Mr. Browning will come without excuses." It seems probable that he guessed what was happening but preferred not to know for certain. Robert wanted to tell him outright, but Elizabeth advised against it—rightly, I think:

I know perfectly that either he would be unhappy himself, or he would make us so. He never could bear the sense of responsibility. Then, as he told me today, and as long ago I knew . . he's "irresolute," timid in deciding. Then he shrinks before the daemon of the World—and "What may be said" is louder to him than thunder.

Knowing, too, that, when they did get married, anyone who seemed to have had foreknowledge would be cast by her father into outer darkness, she was anxious to keep the number as small as possible. Her sisters had to know, but neither her brothers nor Robert's parents. She did confide in Mr. Gould, her former Greek teacher, who had long been blind. An old servant of her grandparents, Trippy, a real Creole mammy, who disapproved of Emancipation and dined at Wimpole Street every Sunday, had guessed, and so, of course, had her personal maid, Elizabeth Wilson. Trippy was too old and too privileged to suffer, but Wilson

The Museum of Modern Art
Christmas catalogue

An illustrated, 40-page catalogue presenting new cards and constructions, books, posters, reproductions, and a wide selection of distinctive gifts from The Museum of Modern Art is now available. Cards and constructions—15 cents to $1—reproduce classic works by artists in the Museum collection. Others have been specially commissioned from such artists as Jean-Michel Folon and Robert Indiana. Gifts ranging from $2.50 to $500 include a special edition of *Playplax;* the *1971 Appointment Calendar; Float,* Robert Breer's intriguing kinetic sculpture; *The Ball Puzzle,* Charles Perry's exquisite lucite object: *Typewriter Eraser,* a signed and numbered offset lithograph by Claes Oldenburg; *Planetary Folklore Participations No. 1,* Victor Vasarely's exciting game in which the player can move magnetized pieces to create any design; and the *Trova Kaleidoscope*—an unusual version of a classic Christmas toy.

The Museum of Modern Art 001
5300 Lenox Hill Station
New York, New York 10021

I enclose 25c for the 1970 Christmas catalogue

Name

Address

figure 5.65

figure 5.66

figure 5.67

***figure* 5.65** Eisenberg Ice Dog Collar. *The New Yorker*, c. 1970.

***figure* 5.66** *The New Yorker.*

***figure* 5.67** Velvet Dog Collar with two pavé-set circles with pavé-set V's on black satin, made in the 1970s. Fastens in the back. No Eisenberg markings. 1" wide x 17" long.

Changing with the Times

The Post-Sterling World

In 1947, Eisenberg & Sons began allowing stores to carry just their jewelry and cosmetics lines. This was the first time they separated these two product lines from the clothing. A potentially profitable move, it dramatically increased the amount of jewelry they would buy from F&K.

At the time, the use of sterling ended and rhodium became the dominant manufacturing metal for costume jewelry. Rhodium is a non-tarnishing, lightweight, super-shiny silver metal. The move to rhodium after the war was immediate. Rhodium is still used today, often over sterling, to help retain the shine.

European stones and crystals were also beginning to become available again. This meant that F&K could go back to the superior stones they had been missing during the war. However, there would be a decrease in the use of the large stones and the size of the jewelry in general.

Eisenberg was partly following fashion trends and partly giving in to the demands of mass production. The complicated designs of the Originals years could never have been produced at the new market prices. Yet there were also advantages in the material changes that allowed stones to be set much tighter, bringing down the overall size of the finished pieces.

figure 6.1 Purple Dimensional Clip Earrings. Marked Block Eisenberg. In 1957 ad. Rhodium. Gorgeous purple marquis rhinestones are joined and stacked. Pavé set clear rhinestones surround a center purple accent stone. *Courtesy of The Erin Byrne Buffaline Collection.*

figure 6.2 Source unknown. Suburban period, late 1940s.

figure 6.3 Source unknown, c. 1950.

figure 6.4

Likewise, it was no longer practical to make pieces with ten different sized and cut stones. Designs needed to be simple, done with one or two stone varieties and only a few colors per piece. Kamke worked hard to keep the designs interesting, and a half-moon arc of pavé stones became a common signature. Yet by the 1950s it had become much harder to spot an Eisenberg piece amidst the array of similar jewelry on the market. Some unusual pieces appeared in the Suburban line. Introduced in 1949 to enhance sporty clothing, they eliminated obvious glitter and included chains, tassels, and simple metal designs. Metal, beads, and glass would dominate, accented with rhinestones.

F&K fought to stay competitive as technical advances lowered the cost of jewelry made in Rhode Island. The company also came under new management when Florence Nathan Silverman and her husband, Murray Silverman, purchased the company. Many collectors feel these later pieces don't match the design quality of the Originals years. Yet in the field of costume jewelry of the 1950s, Eisenberg's creations are considered top notch. Even after F&K abandoned handset prong-held stones in favor of glued settings, Eisenberg jewelry was still revered.

Kamke continued to design well-received pieces and even continued the figurals. Despite its struggles, F&K was still using only the finest imported stones and crystals, and its work from this period was considered finer than the other jewelry in the stores that carried it, though these were no longer exclusively high-end retailers.

figure 6.4 Rhinestone Necklace. Marked Block Eisenberg, c. 1950s. Rhodium. Clear round rhinestones with a two accent pieces flanking a center drop with a large clear oval ringed by clear marquis petals. Pavé set clears run in ribbons. Necklace 20," decoration 1⅞" × 1⅜". *Courtesy of Jaedra Theriault.*

figure 6.5

figure 6.6

figure 6.7

figure 6.8

figure 6.5 Bead Tassel Bracelet. Marked Block Eisenberg, c. 1950. Luminescent blue beads are strung singly or in pairs accented with gold filigree caps with a line of clear rhinestones. A golden chandelier tassel has a large center bead and a pendant drop, both accented with clear rhinestone rows. 8" long.

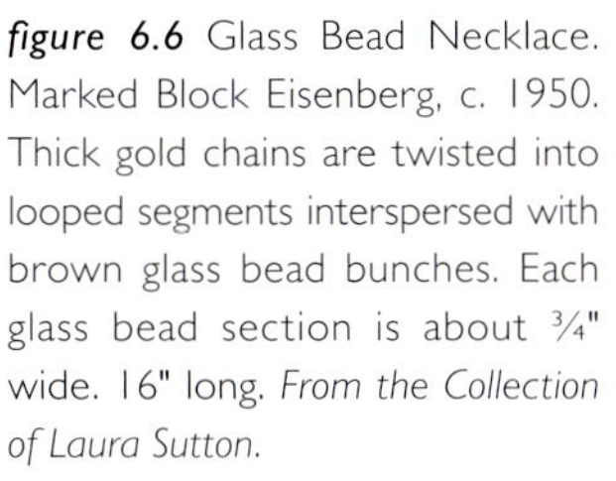

figure 6.6 Glass Bead Necklace. Marked Block Eisenberg, c. 1950. Thick gold chains are twisted into looped segments interspersed with brown glass bead bunches. Each glass bead section is about ¾" wide. 16" long. *From the Collection of Laura Sutton.*

figure 6.7 Floral Brooch. Marked Block Eisenberg, c. 1950s. Rhodium. Dimensional floral design with marquis, round, and teardrop clear rhinestones. The clear center rhinestone is accented with two twisting ribbon loops of pavé set clear rhinestones. *Courtesy of The Erin Byrne Buffaline Collection.*

figure 6.8 Cascading Floral Brooch. Marked Block E, c. 1950s. Rhodium. Round, marquis, and oval clear rhinestones form the flower. Draping vines are set above the rest of the design and accented with multiple cuts of clears. Pavé and bezel set clears add accent. 3¼" × 1¾."

figure 6.9 Source unknown, c. 1953.

The 1950s saw the Eisenberg Original mark gone from the jewelry forever. The marks that follow were varied and seem to have no definite time period. Our assessment of these pieces shows that four marks followed the sterling Eisenberg Originals. They appear in this general order – Script E, used even earlier if space on a piece was limited; Script Eisenberg; Block Eisenberg; and Block E. These marks overlap, and some nearly identical designs are marked differently. No pieces in this period were marked ICE. There are, however, some sterling pieces marked Block E and some early rhodium pieces marked Original.

figure 6.10 Amethyst Choker Necklace. Marked Eisenberg in script, late 1940s. The gold structure forms an interesting crosshatch pattern with each end point capped in an amethyst rhinestone. A center line of larger raised amethyst stones cover the crossover points with large amethyst drops along the bottom. 14½" × 1¼".

figure 6.11

figure 6.12

figure 6.13

figure 6.11 Clear drop earrings. Clip back with beveled round stone at top. Hinged to hold pear-shaped rhinestone. No markings. 1" × ⅜".

figure 6.12 Pink Rhinestone Drop Earrings. Marked Block Eisenberg, c. 1950s. Multiple hues of pink rhinestones form two swinging drops and are set in rhodium. Lines of pavé set clears run throughout. Clip Backs. 2⅛" × ⅝".

figure 6.13 Green and Citrine Floral Earrings. Marked Block Eisenberg, c. 1950s. Deep emerald-green round rhinestones make up the petals with a large yellow round layered on top. Two yellow marquis stones form leaves accented with clear pavé set rhinestones. 1½" × ¾". *From the Collection of Laura Sutton.*

figure 6.14

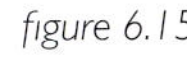

figure 6.15

figure 6.16

figure 6.17

figure 6.14 Articulated Drop Earrings. Marked Block E, c. 1950. Rhodium. Screw back. A large round clear rhinestone anchors a drop banded in matching round clear rhinestones. Two half-moons set with clear pavé rhinestones crisscross in the center. *Courtesy of The Erin Byrne Buffaline Collection.*

figure 6.15 Art Deco Overlapping Crystal Bracelet. Marked Script E. Shown in 1951 ad. Rhodium. Two bands of faceted prong set stones cross at the center of the wrist and end in oval anchor stones. 8½" × ½".

figure 6.16 Rhinestone Necklace. Marked Block Eisenberg, c. 1950s. Done with clear rhinestones this graduating necklace has a center section of clear round rhinestones holding nine drops, five of which are teardrops. *Courtesy of The Erin Byrne Buffaline Collection.*

figure 6.17 Blue and White Deco Dress Clip. Marked Script E, late 1940s. Rhodium. A large clear faceted top stone perches above three layers of small blue faceted square rhinestones in "V" formations. 2½" × 1¾".

figure 6.18

figure 6.19

figure 6.20

figure 6.21

figure 6.18 Citrine and Clear Rhinestone Clip Earrings. Marked Script E, c. 1950. Golden based with clear crystal stones topped with fans made of six marquis-shaped citrine rhinestones. 1¼" × 1¾".

figure 6.19 Petite Rhinestone Clip Earrings. Marked Eisenberg, c. 1950s. One emerald-cut clear rhinestone with a smaller clear round accent piece on bottom. These earrings were found with the Eisenberg locket, though were likely purchased later to complement it. ¾" × ½".

figure 6.20 Deco Clip Earrings. Marked Block Eisenberg, c. 1950s. Stacked clear emerald-cut rhinestones. 1" × ¾".

figure 6.21 Two-Tone Rhinestone Brooch. Marked Block Eisenberg, c. 1950. Rhodium. A freeform shape done with dark cobalt blue and light baby blue rhinestones. The design is banded by a curving strand of clear pavé set rhinestones. 2" × 2".

I dreamed I was a Lady Ambassador in my*

**maidenform bra®*

figure 6.22 Maidenform bra advertisement from the 1950s featuring iconic Eisenberg eagle and earrings.

Shown: Maidenform's Maidenette* in white satin and lace . . . from 1.50   There is a *maidenform* for every type of figure!

*REG. U. S. PAT. OFF.   COSTUME: ALAN GRAHAM   HAT: MR. JOHN   JEWELS: EISENBERG

By the end of the 1950s, Eisenberg Original no longer applied to any aspect of the company.

A large eagle brooch led a glamorous life, shown on the right. Actress Thelma Ritter wore it prominently in the 1953 version of *Titanic*. It was spotlighted in a Maidenform bra advertisement. And it was a featured piece the summer it was released. The matching eagle earrings are quite rare and have a slightly different appearance.

figure 6.23

figure 6.24

figure 6.25

figure 6.23 Rare Iconic Eagle. Marked Script Eisenberg, c. 1950s. Rhodium base with bezel set center stone. Pavé set clears cover the layered feathers on the body and wings. Large clear navettes imitating draping feathers hang from the wings. 3¾" × 2⅜".

figure 6.24 Rare eagle earrings, 1950s, rhodium base with pear-shaped bezel stones on wings. 1¼" × 1".

figure 6.25 Small Eagle Brooch. Marked Script Eisenberg, 1950s. Rhodium with clear center stone. Clear pavé set stones cover the body and wings with clear navette stones draping for feathers. Design is similar but altered from the larger version. 2¼" × 2¼".

figure 6.26 Advertisement, c. 1950s. Iconic large eagle featured by Bergdorf Goodman. Source unknown.

Beads and Brilliance—

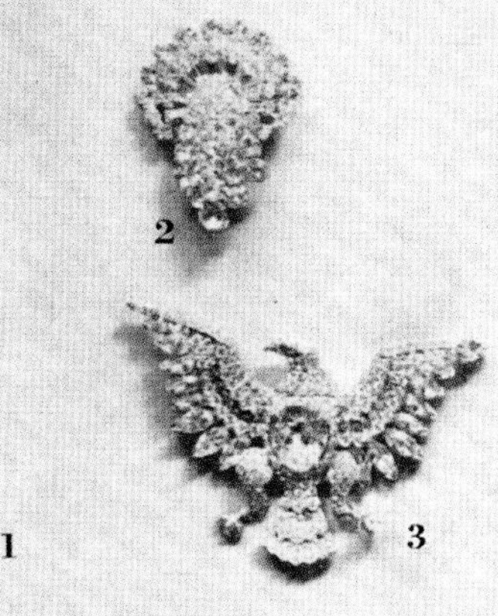

• This is the year when the flood of summer jeweling runs in two clear and cogent channels—two separate schools. Beads, for one: great splashing rivers of them, pearly, chalky, gilded, to wear in ropes by day with shirts and sun dresses, looped in shining bibs with the bare-shouldered prints of evening. The other school? A brilliant one, jeweling a sleeve or a starchy organdie beret with diamanté glitter; dazzling, after dark, in the delicate lace-patterned necklace.

1. Tiny chalky white saucer beads, strung together here in a lei of sixty-inch ropes. By Trifari. About $15* each. Saks Fifth Avenue.

2. The new summer astronomy—rhinestones showered from a star, to pin on a sweater, decorate a shirt cuff. By Kramer. About $10.* Saks Fifth Avenue.

3. A familiar eagle—emblazoned now in brilliants. By Eisenberg. About $45.* Bergdorf Goodman.

4. And a new "floating" jewel: colored stones, tasseled out in airy arabesques by designer Charles James to follow the contours of your throat. About $70.* Lord and Taylor.

5

figure 6.27

figure 6.28

figure 6.29

figure 6.27 *Vogue*–September 1, 1955.

figure 6.28 Floral Brooch. Marked Block Eisenberg. Shown in 1955 ad. Rhodium. Four layered open petals of clear emerald-cut rhinestones, two with clear teardrop centers are interspersed with tiny clear accents. Stem is clear square-cut rhinestones. 3" × 2¼". *Courtesy of Carmen Robertson / Carmen's Collectibles.*

figure 6.29 Bouquet of Teardrops Brooch. Marked Block Eisenberg, c. 1950s. Center section of clear rounds lined with pavé set clears. Both sides are dimensional rows of faceted clear teardrop rhinestones. 2" × 2½".

figure 6.30 Vogue, October 1, 1956.

During the 1950s, Eisenberg experimented with new materials. Kamke, still designing, used poured, blown, and molded glass pieces. Heart designs were being advertised along with new forms of animals. Starburst brooch and floral earrings were interesting designs. Luminescent cabochons and aurora borealis stones (named after the Northern Lights) enhanced these designs.

figure 6.31

figure 6.32

figure 6.31 Glass Bubble Fur Clip. Marked Eisenberg, c. 1950. Fascinating translucent glass beads in amber hues including yellow, cherry, and warm honey are piled together in a dimensional array. Clear round and emerald-cut rhinestones of various sizes are tucked within. 1¾" × 1½". *From the Collection of Laura Sutton.*

figure 6.32 Mauve and Clear Rhinestone Brooch. Marked with Script E, c. 1950. Three large clear accent stones surround a band of mauve stones. Highlighted by a cluster of mauve glass beads interspersed with clear faux pearls. 1½" × 1".

figure 6.33 Bouquet Brooch. Marked Eisenberg Original, c. 1948. Gold metal, possibly washed rhodium. Lemon faceted pear stone forms the vase with wired yellow glass beads blooming above, some of which are actually figural flowers. Faceted round rhinestones add accent. 2" × 1¾" × 1¾" thick.

figure 6.34 *Vogue*, March 1, 1957.

figure 6.35

figure 6.37

figure 6.36

figure 6.35 Milk Glass Necklace. Marked Block Eisenberg, c. 1950s. Rhodium-set milk glass stones hug the neck with a rhinestone extender at the clasp. The centerpiece is white milk glass stones fanning down from light blue rhinestone anchors. The Eisenberg arc of clear pavé sets add accent. 16" × $1\frac{1}{4}$".

figure 6.36 Milk Glass Brooch. Marked Block Eisenberg, c. 1950s. Rhodium-set white milk glass stones arc across the top of the piece while three cascading stone ribbons dangle from the bottom. Clear rhinestones run along the center. $2\frac{1}{2}$" × $1\frac{3}{8}$".

figure 6.37 Milk Glass Earrings. Marked Block Eisenberg, c. 1950s. Golden metal swirls hold clear rhinestones while large milk glass stones anchor the design. Clip Backs. $\frac{7}{8}$" × $\frac{1}{2}$".

figure 6.38 *Vogue*, September 15, 1948.

figure 6.39

figure 6.40

figure 6.41

figure 6.39 Articulated Heart Brooch. Marked Block Eisenberg, shown in 1948 ad. Rhodium. Figural heart outlined with small clear rhinestones. Tiny crown-like peaks run along the outside with three small, clear stones. Huge, ¾" clear faceted pendant swings freely. 2" × 2". *Courtesy of Carmen Robertson / Carmen's Collectibles.*

figure 6.40 Heart Brooch. Marked Eisenberg, c. 1950. Rhodium. Heart is 1" long and covered with pavé set clears surrounding a large inset clear. A bouquet blooms above with flowers of rounds and pavé petals. Various clear rounds decorate the rest of the spray. 2½" × 2¼". *From the Collection of Laura Sutton.*

figure 6.41 Heart Earrings. Marked Script E, c. 1950. Found with heart brooch. Rhodium. Large center clears are surrounded by heart-shaped framing bearing small clears. Screw back. ½" ×¾". *From the Collection of Laura Sutton.*

figure 6.42

figure 6.43

figure 6.44

figure 6.45

figure 6.42 Duck Brooch. Marked Eisenberg, c. 1950. Rhodium. Dimensional design with the body, wings, and tail covered by small clears. Perch is done with small clears underlined with five large rounds. A large, sparkling clear sits at the beak. 1¼" × 1¾.

figure 6.43 Owl Brooch. Marked Block E, c. 1950. Rhodium. The body of the owl is done with pavé set clears in lines divided by open space to add definition. Green rhinestones are set as the eyes. 1¾" × 1". *From the Collection of Laura Sutton.*

figure 6.44 Lion Brooch. Marked Block E, c. 1950s. Rhodium. Striking lion's face rises from an elaborate mane. Entire piece is covered in tiny, clear pavé set rhinestones. Careful design defines the features of the face and two tiny green rhinestones are the eyes. 1½" × 1½".

figure 6.45 Fly Brooch. Marked Script E, c. 1950s. Rhodium. The wings are triangular clear rhinestones outlined in clear pavé sets. The body is a clear marquis stone with clear pavé sets. Perch is a large round clear wrapped in a line of pavé set clears. Red enamel accents. 1" × 1¾".

figure 6.46

figure 6.47

figure 6.48

figure 6.46 Iridescent Clip Earrings. Marked Block E, c. 1950. Rhodium. The stunning center stone glows pink with striations of purple. The top is lined with pavé set clears, as is the cabochon. A light blue rhinestone hangs above the drop with three grouped below. 1½" × ½". *From the Collection of Laura Sutton.*

figure 6.47 Cabochon Earrings. Marked Block E, c. 1950s. These earrings share the same lighter-colored, multi-hued glowing stone as the pendant and are also accented with small purple rhinestones. The outline is done with pavé set clears. 1" × ½". *From the Collection of Laura Sutton.*

figure 6.48 Cabochon Pendant. Marked Block Eisenberg, c. 1950s. Antiqued gold metal pavé set lines frame the design. Triangles of tiny purple rhinestones outline the outer edges and hold the sparkling, rainbow-filled center glass stone. 2¼" × ½". *From the Collection of Laura Sutton.*

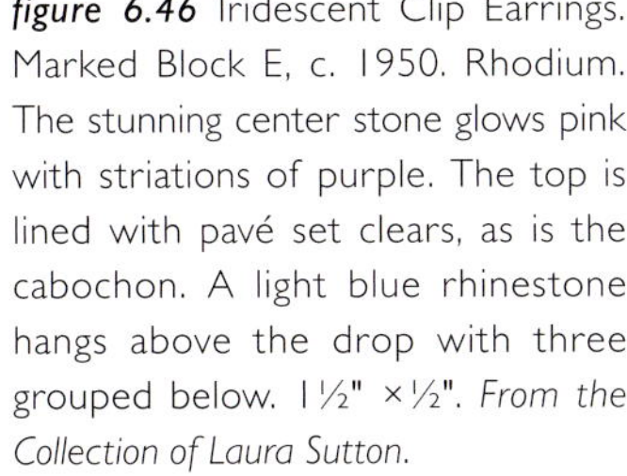

figure 6.49

figure 6.50

figure 6.51

figure 6.52

figure 6.49 Aurora Borealis Brooch. Marked Block E, late 1950s. A stunning array of deep blue marquis stones fan from a raised center section lined with borealis rhinestones. The borealis stones also accent the bottom row and glow with iridescent shades of green and blue. 2" × 3¼". *From the Collection of Laura Sutton.*

figure 6.50 Aurora Borealis Clip Earrings. Marked Block E, late 1950s. Matching blue marquis stones rest amid an outline of borealis stones sharing the same iridescent blue green glow. 1¼" × 1". *From the Collection of Laura Sutton.*

figure 6.51 Yellow "Starburst" Brooch. Marked Eisenberg, c. 1950. Rhodium. The center section is done with clear rhinestones that also center the stars at the end of the arching tines. Open-backed yellow rhinestones tip many of the layered tines. 1¾" × 2¾". *From the Collection of Laura Sutton.*

figure 6.52 Sweeping Floral Earrings. Marked Block E, c. 1950s. Rhodium. Clear rounds of various sizes are clustered together in layers to form the center floral. The stones run along curving and arching metal spokes, many of which are tipped with clear rounds. 2½" × 2". *From the Collection of Laura Sutton.*

In Style

Expanding the Clothing Line

In 1941, Eisenberg & Sons had a revenue of seven figures across the divisions.[1] Yet when they moved into massive accommodations in the Chicago Merchandise Mart, they emblazoned the entrance with a declaration that they were still at heart "Dressmakers." (See fig. 7.6.)

figure 7.1 Pink and Black Dress. Labeled Eisenberg & Sons Original, c. 1930s. Pink silk bodice over black rayon crepe floor-length body with fitted empire waist. Detailing of woven pink silk ribbon that defines the crossover V-neck bodice and bands the puffed cap sleeves. *From the Collection of Joanna van Ritbergen.*

figure 7.2 Rear view showing the woven band of pink silk ribbon that hugs the neck, highlighting the open back, and then bands the natural waist. The puffed cap sleeves add interest to the silhouette. *From the Collection of Joanna van Ritbergen.*

figure 7.1 (above) and figure 7.2 (left)

figure 7.3

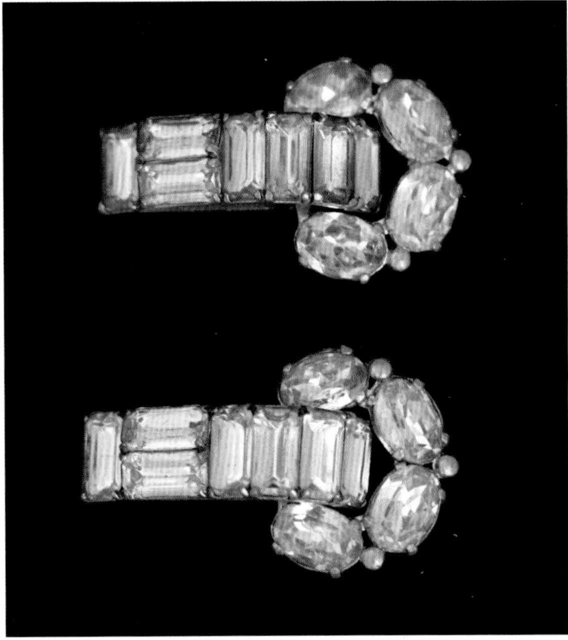

figure 7.4

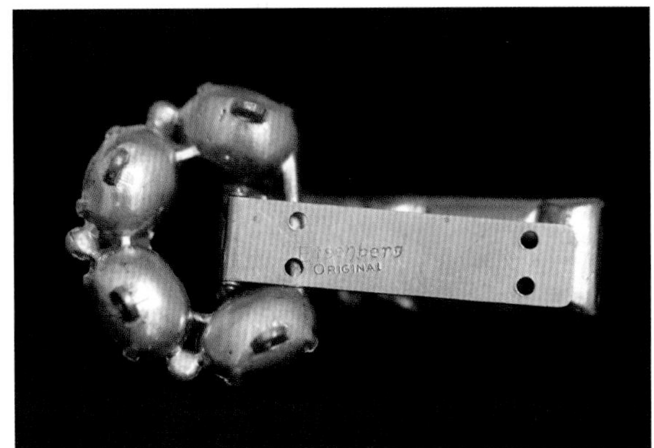

figure 7.5

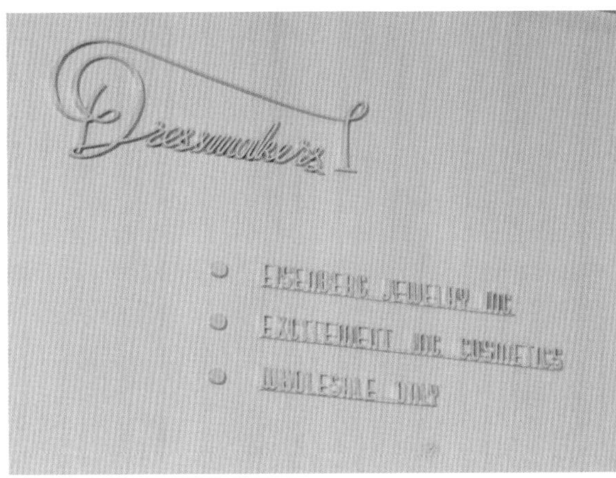

figure 7.6

figure 7.3 *Vogue*, c. 1940. Ad showcases the continued use of jeweled pieces within the clothing line and highlights "how the dresses and the jewelry were made for each other."

figure 7.4 Pair of Buckle Sew-Ons. Marked Eisenberg Original, c. 1940s. Shown in advertisement on original jacket. End loops are done with clear oval-cut stones and the bars are done in clear emerald-cut stones. 3" × 3¼". *From the Collection of Joanna van Ritbergen.*

figure 7.5 Rear view of sew-on buckles showing holes for attaching as well as the Eisenberg Original mark. *From the Collection of Joanna van Ritbergen.*

figure 7.6 Eisenberg Shop in Chicago, November 19, 1941. Chicago History Museum. *Photo by Hedrich-Blessing.*

figure 7.7

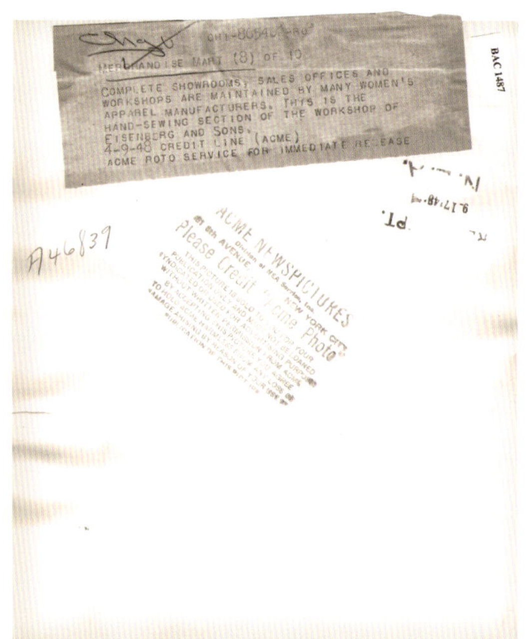

figure 7.8

figure 7.9

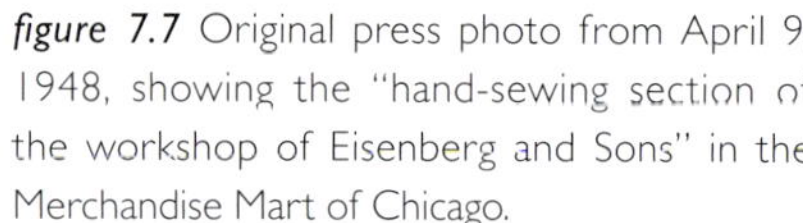

figure 7.7 Original press photo from April 9, 1948, showing the "hand-sewing section of the workshop of Eisenberg and Sons" in the Merchandise Mart of Chicago.

figure 7.9 Black crepe cocktail dress c. 1940s. Asymmetrical keyhole neckline outlined with elaborate, rust-colored beading with a large sunburst and green stone center. Draping front and dipping hem.

figure 7.8 Back of Photo. Acme Newspapers, Div. of NEA Services Inc., New York, 9-17-1948.

figure 7.10 Close-up of beaded neckline.

figure 7.10

figure 7.11

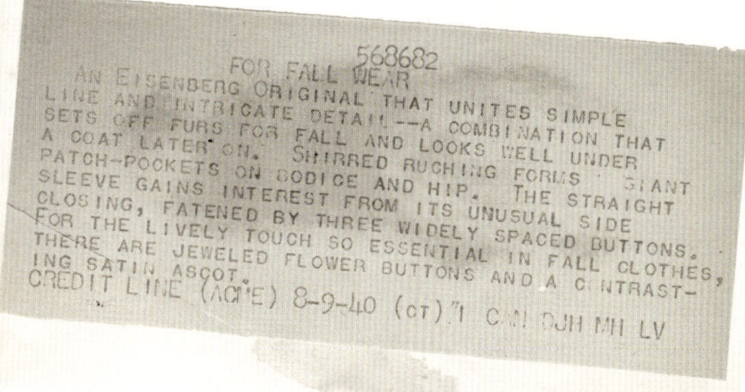

568682
FOR FALL WEAR
AN EISENBERG ORIGINAL THAT UNITES SIMPLE
LINE AND INTRICATE DETAIL--A COMBINATION THAT
SETS OFF FURS FOR FALL AND LOOKS WELL UNDER
A COAT LATER ON. SHIRRED RUCHING FORMS GIANT
PATCH-POCKETS ON BODICE AND HIP. THE STRAIGHT
SLEEVE GAINS INTEREST FROM ITS UNUSUAL SIDE
CLOSING, FATENED BY THREE WIDELY SPACED BUTTONS.
FOR THE LIVELY TOUCH SO ESSENTIAL IN FALL CLOTHES,
THERE ARE JEWELED FLOWER BUTTONS AND A CONTRAST-
ING SATIN ASCOT.
CREDIT LINE (ACME) 8-9-40 (CT) "1 CM DJH MH LV

figure 7.12

figure 7.11 Original 1940 Eisenberg press photo showcases a detailed ensemble featuring elaborate jeweled buttons.

figure 7.12 Back of press photo. 8-9-40. Acme Newspapers, Inc. Quoted "For Fall Wear . . . An Eisenberg Original that unites simple line and intricate detail—a combination that sets off furs for fall and looks well under a coat later on. Shirred ruching forms giant patch-pockets on bodice and hip. The straight sleeve gains interest from its unusual side closing, fastened by three widely spaced buttons. For the lively touch so essential in fall clothes, there are jeweled flower buttons and a contrast-satin ascot."

***figure 7.13** & **figure 7.14** Vogue*, May 1937. *From the Collection of Laura Sutton.*

— around the clock in Suwanee Ensembles. Happy summer to them! With places to go — and things to do — the way they look means, oh! so much! Any evening — any afternoon — any morning — here are the cotton dresses they'll need. All cleanable and color-fast. Just wear and wear and tub and tub — to the end of a perfect summer. But now, the important thing is the skilful handling of the dressmaker features identical with the best hand-needled Eisenberg dresses! Yes — you'll find them in America's finer stores — or Address Eisenberg and Sons, Dressmakers, 847 West Jackson Boulevard, Chicago.

Eisenberg & Sons added coats and ensembles to their clothing line, as well as practical wear to satisfy changing consumer demands and increase market share. While evening wear was still popular, women wanted more practical pieces. The Suwanee Ensembles label contained the same devotion to excellence and detailing as the Originals label, but these garments were made from more durable materials and with color-fast dyes.

figure 7.15

figure 7.16

figure 7.17

figure 7.15 Coral Pink Dress. Labeled Suwanee Ensembles Original Eisenberg & Sons, late 1930s. Cotton delight with a white lace scalloped neckline with decorative piping over a tucked bodice. Has a fitted waist to a full, floor-length skirt. Lace and piping also band the cap sleeves. *From the Collection of Joanna van Ritbergen.*

figure 7.16 Rear view showing a mostly bare back is outlined with a small band of white lace and swirls of decorative piping. Tiny decorative buttons decorate the sides and meet to run into the skirt. Tucked waist. *From the Collection of Joanna van Ritbergen*

figure 7.17 Early version of the Suwanee Ensembles label. *From the Collection of Joanna van Ritbergen.*

figure 7.18 *Eisenberg & Sons* catalog, copyright 1944. Page prepared by *Abbott Kimball Co.* Describes the need for attractive and purposeful fashions even during war years. Eisenberg Originals illustration of 1944 fashion and jewelry for Joseph Spiess, Elgin, Illinois. (Unidentified illustrator.) *Courtesy of D. Brett Benson, Inc. West Palm Beach, FL.*

INTO *the fourth winter of war...now every part of your life, every one of your possessions has meaning—purpose—a clearly defined usefulness. Your time is dedicated to helping shorten the war...your money to helping win the war. You have no patience with waste...extravagance...non-essentials.*

YOUR wardrobe mirrors your new purposefulness. You measure every addition by the rigid yardstick..."What does it do for me? How does it fit into my life?" You demand that your clothes be practical; but you recognize that to maintain your own beauty, your own distinction, is to maintain a bulwark against all the change ...all the conflict about you. To your family...to your man... you remain the serene and lovely center of a stormy world.

IT IS with an understanding of this need in your life that EISENBERG has designed these clothes for you. We are proud to present this Fall Collection of EISENBERG ORIGINALS FOR 1944. They're feminine, lovely clothes...dedicated to the simplicity that best underlines your completely American beauty... but, above all, they're clothes that have purpose.

HATS BY Peg Fischer

PREPARED BY ABBOTT KIMBALL CO.

Eisenberg & Sons
ORIGINAL
Eisenberg Originals in a special Onondaga sheer. Shown at finer stores throughout America. Write Eisenberg & Sons, 847 West Jackson Boulevard, Chicago, Illinois, for the name of the store nearest you. ★★★★
HATS BY LILLY DACHÉ

figure 7.19

figure 7.20

figure 7.19 *Vogue*, February 1, 1940. The dress on the right bears Eisenberg's favorite white lace detailing. The ensemble on the model on the left has large decorative buttons.

figure 7.20 *Vogue*, February 1, 1941. This is all about the white lace detailing. "Ruffles of Spring for your first black dress."

figure 7.21

In contrast to Eisenberg & Sons Original's famous silk creations, the Suwanee Ensembles pieces were easily washed and maintained. The label was advertised separately throughout its life. Suwanee Ensembles labels included the wording Eisenberg Original or Eisenberg & Sons.

It is interesting to see the variation between the two labels that are only a few years apart. The last ad for the Suwanee Ensembles label in *Vogue* that we found was May 15, 1945. By then the Eisenberg & Sons Originals label included pieces made of more hardy materials and there would have been little need for a separate line.

An announcement in *Women's Wear Daily* on October 30, 1942, introduces the new collection of Eisenberg Originals. There are clothing pieces dating from later in the 1940s that clearly still have the Original label, but increasingly in advertising, and on the accessories, the new moniker would be used. Eventually it would be the only phrasing used across the lines and labels. Stores begin to highlight that they were carrying these Eisenberg lines in their stores.

Colored accents, contrasting colors, and the ever-present embellishments were highlights of Eisenberg & Sons' first New York press showing in 1945.

figure 7.22

figure 7.23

The review of the Eisenberg Originals line printed in *Women's Wear Daily* on June 13, 1945, states "Attention to detail in contour and fit distinguishes this group, in which the two-piece theme is refreshingly handled, through encrustations which promote color contrast."

The review went on to say, "Particularly original is the use of bright emerald and royal blue scrolls set into the left shoulder and opposite hip in black, this idea matched by the jacket lining, half blue, half green."

"Sequins, silvery nail heads, and embroidery of gilt spangles" were also mentioned.

figure 7.24

***figure* 7.21** Cotton Dress. Labeled Suwanee Ensembles by Eisenberg & Sons, c. 1940s. Made in a black-and-white gingham check accented across the bodice with groupings of multi-colored sequins. *From the Collection of Laura Sutton.*

***figure* 7.22** Close-up of sequined bodice. *From the Collection of Laura Sutton.*

***figure* 7.23** Later version of the Suwanee Ensembles label. *From the Collection of Laura Sutton.*

***figure* 7.24** Source unknown, c. 1943. A store ad highlighting Eisenberg Originals. The dress is "white shantung richly embroidered from cape to hemline." Eisenberg's Excitement fragrance and several pieces of sterling jewelry are also showcased.

figure 7.26

figure 7.25

figure 7.25 Black Rayon Crepe Dress. Labeled Eisenberg & Sons Original, c. 1940s. Sexy, deep V-neck with bodice tailoring. Fitted skirt. Two long panels drape from the waist and are elaborately beaded with gold sequin scrollwork. The patterned gold sequins are repeated on the shoulders.

figure 7.26 Source unknown, September 1946. Store ad showing an Eisenberg wool suit with elaborate gold embroidery. Matching embroidery decorates the rayon crepe blouse beneath. Located in the "Designer's Shop" of Jordan Marsh.

figure 7.27

figure 7.28

figure 7.29

figure 7.27 Source unknown, c. 1946. Lasalle's of Toledo store advertisement showing an Eisenberg suit finished with long lines of buttons down the back and along the sides. The front of the suit is shown in the picture hanging on the wall. *From the Collection of Laura Sutton.*

figure 7.28 Heavily Beaded Black Rayon Crepe Cocktail Dress. Labeled Eisenberg & Sons Original, c. 1940s. Dress has a deeply dropped waist and the elongated bodice is covered with countless tiny black glass beads forming elaborate floral patterns. Beading continues down the three-quarter-length sleeves.

figure 7.29 Close-up of floral patterned beading.

figure 7.30

figure 7.31

figure 7.32

figure 7.30 *Vogue*, March 1947. This fall ensemble featured a jacket lined with a bold print at the collar and cuffs. Matching patterning enhances the blouse beneath.

figure 7.31 Wool Coat. Labeled Eisenberg & Sons Original, c. 1940s. Winter practicality is augmented with style in this elegant swing coat that closes with two ornate decorative buttons. The coat is enhanced by a splash of color from an Eisenberg Original scarf.

figure 7.32 Close-up of decorative buttons.

figure 7.35

figure 7.33

figure 7.34

figure 7.36

***figure* 7.33** Elaborate Sleeved Dress. Labeled Eisenberg & Sons Original, featured in 1947 ad. Black rayon crepe dress with flowing sleeves. Same fabric is piled in ruffled rows at sleeve ends and in a band at the hips. *From the Collection of Joanna van Ritbergen.*

***figure* 7.34** Source unknown, early 1950s. Advertisement of Eisenberg's trademark sheath. *From Joske's of Texas, San Antonio.*

***figure* 7.35** The elongated sleeve cuff is shown draped across the body. *From the Collection of Joanna van Ritbergen.*

***figure* 7.36** *Vogue*, c. 1948. Flowing sleeves and band at hip covered in ruffled rows of crepe. *From the Collection of Joanna van Ritbergen.*

In 1948 Eisenberg launched its first and only cross-over line named Suburban, which included perfume, clothing, and jewelry. On December 30, 1948, *Women's Wear Daily* noted that the seasonal launch of the new clothing series was "a response to a need for quality classics with softer touches." The first collection focused on "coat dresses and jacket suits, always presenting them in a good sturdy fabric that can take hard wear, notably worsteds." The highlighted beige Forstmann gabardine dress cost $110. The company itself referred to the "Eisenberg Suburban" line as "proud, polished classics tailored for fashion stamina." We have found examples of the Suburban fragrance and jewelry, but have never seen a Suburban-label piece of clothing outside of the advertising.

figure 7.37

figure 7.38

figure 7.37 *Vogue*, c. 1948. Dreamy artist-drawn advertisement for Eisenberg Originals.

figure 7.38 Source Unknown, c.1948. A stylish artist-drawn store ad for Eisenberg from Emma Lange, Inc. Milwaukee.

figure 7.39 *Vogue*, April 15, 1949. This ad showcases a lipstick perfumed with the new Suburban fragrance. Other Suburban cosmetic products are also shown, along with a glimpse of the clothing and jewelry. *From the Collection of Joanna van Ritbergen.*

figure 7.40 Source unknown, c. 1950. Magnificent beaded appliqué enhances the lapel of this tailored wool suit. The beaded pattern is repeated on the rayon satin blouse.

figure 7.40

figure 7.39

As the 1940s ended and Eisenberg was becoming known for its jewelry, its clothing was still singled out in reviews for its detailing and impeccable design. The beginning of the 1950s saw Eisenberg relocate once again, this time to 22 West Madison, Chicago. The new space featured 50,000 square feet of showrooms and workrooms and was believed to have the "largest better dress factory in the country" according to a write-up in the January 10, 1950, issue of *Women's Wear Daily*.

The new location also housed a new enterprise. According to an article in *Women's Wear Daily* on February 1, 1950, a fashion library was slated to open in April that year. The plan was to give designers and advanced fashion students access to Chicago's first fashion and costume archives. A full-time librarian was planned for the nonprofit enterprise, and its founding was aided by the contribution of hundreds of rare books on loan from Fairchild Publications, the publisher of *Women's Wear Daily*.

The clothing was doing so well that the company hired the most well-known model of her time, Jean Patchett, and beading, embellishments, lace, and accent details continued to enhance the designs.

figure 7.41

figure 7.42

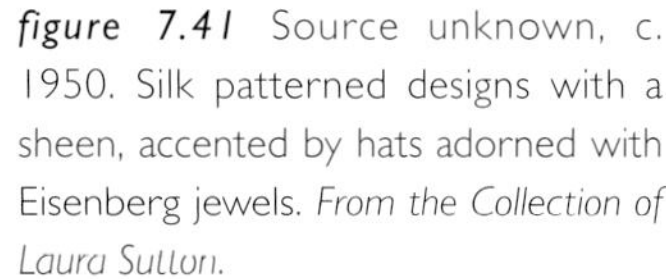

figure 7.41 Source unknown, c. 1950. Silk patterned designs with a sheen, accented by hats adorned with Eisenberg jewels. *From the Collection of Laura Sutton.*

figure 7.42 Source unknown, c. 1951. Striking detailing in both color and decoration make this suit pop. The ad stated that the rayon blouse beneath bears the same styling. *From the Collection of Laura Sutton.*

figure 7.43 *Vogue*, August 1949. A stylish and creative photographic ad showcasing Eisenberg Originals dresses of rayon crepe with applied satin detailing. Timeless yet distinctive.

In 1958, Eisenberg announced the end of the clothing line. The label had been hurt with the proliferation of Eisenberg jewelry into more mainstream outlets. The many product lines of the 1940s had been retired, and Eisenberg Originals' most loyal clients were aging. Still, sales were reportedly strong and the collections were well reviewed. However, the clothing also was a heavier investment than the flourishing jewelry line.

The industry was taken aback by the sudden move and lamented the company's decision. It seemed unthinkable that the "Dressmakers of Chicago" would no longer be in the clothing business.

It was the end of a remarkable fashion journey highlighted by exquisite craftsmanship, creative styling, elaborate detailing, and a fierce commitment to quality. The clothing spawned the jewelry for which Eisenberg would become best known, and ultimately it was probably the highly profitable jewelry that killed the Originals.

COFFIN

MEADOW LILIES, those tiny, tawny lilies-of-the-field, on a rayon dress with a star-pointed neckline, its sleeveless brown linen jacket lined in the lily print. About $90. Costume by Eisenberg (the dress, a linen-y fabric by [illegible] of [illegible] rayon), and gilt [illegible] jewellery, at Tailored Woman. The costume, also at The Dayton Co., J. P. Allen; J. W. Robinson. The lipstick and nail polish, both in a fresh shade of flame: "Orange Spice" by Peggy Sage.

124 VOGUE, DECEMBER, 1953

figure 7.44

figure **7.44** *Vogue*, 1953, Lilies-of-the-field patterned dress is teamed with a sleeveless brown linen jacket lined with the same lily print.

figure **7.45** Floral Jacket. Labeled Eisenberg Originals, mid-1950s. Short silk jacket with floral patterning. Closes with rhinestone buckles.

figure **7.46** Close-up view of clear rhinestone buckle that enhances the belted jacket.

figure **7.47** White Lace Dress. Labeled Eisenberg Originals, mid-1950s. Eisenberg's favorite black and white is showcased here in a black silk crepe dress with a white lace bodice accented with rhinestones. Long, wide black crepe ties can be worn in multiple ways.

figure **7.48** Rear view of dress showing the long ties draping down the back at the waist. These can also be pulled up and over to be worn as a shawl.

figure **7.49** Close-up of beading on lace bodice.

figure 7.45

figure 7.46

figure 7.47

figure 7.48

figure 7.49

figure 7.50 Source unknown, c. 1955. The black velvet is beautifully accented by Eisenberg's signature white lace. The wool sheath is accented by silk ruffles at the collar and sleeves.

DRAMA: curtain rising on new after-dark shapes by Eisenberg. Starring you, stealing the show.

Right: Theatre Suit, reed slim, in velvet with white lace, Eisenberg Ice buttons.

Left: Sheath in Forstmann's chiffon wool with pleated pure silk chiffon ruff.

Each $90.

Eisenberg Originals

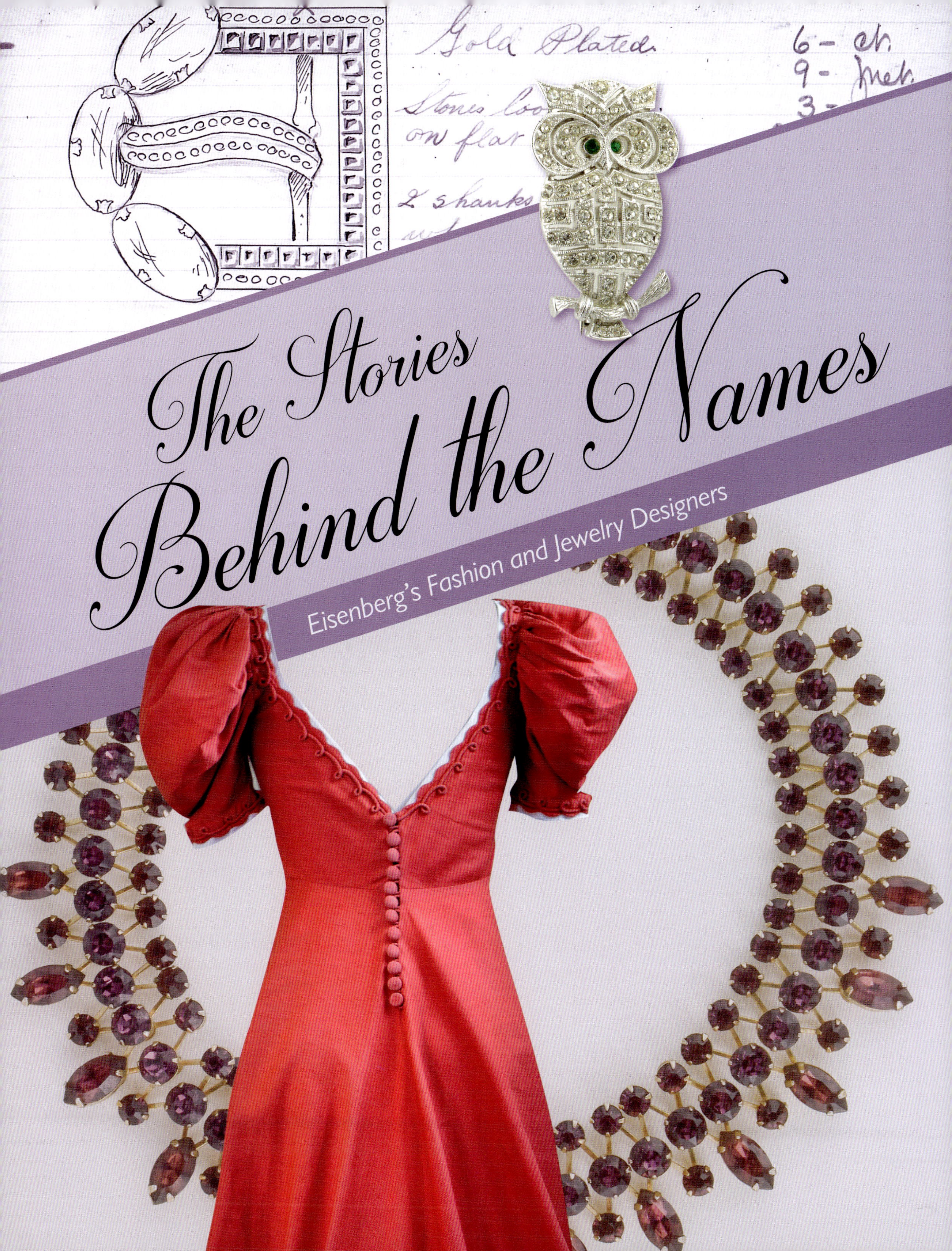
Gold Plated
6 - ch.
9 - Inch.
3 -
Stones loo
on flat
2 shanks
The Stories
Behind the Names
Eisenberg's Fashion and Jewelry Designers

IRMA MARIE KIRCHNER. Born in Austria about 1894, she became Irma Kirby when she married in 1909, and had one daughter. The timeline indicates she would have been about twenty-six when she joined Eisenberg & Sons in 1920. Kirchner would style the Eisenberg & Sons Original label to the heights of the American fashion world.

She also designed limited-edition pieces in the Eisenberg Original label that could be customized for individual patrons. The company rewarded her with a portion of the company and the title of vice president during its incorporation in 1928.

Kirchner left briefly in late 1935 or early 1936, though she retained her share of the company. She is quoted in *Women's Wear Daily* on March 10, 1936, as saying that she believes primarily in putting "things into a dress, not on it." Perhaps she felt her designs were being overshadowed by the Eisenberg's new jewelry line. Or perhaps Eisenberg's expansion beyond clothing was creating friction. Clearly, she felt strongly enough to leave, but not for long.

Within two years she would start her own line, work for two other companies, and then in 1938 she would return to Eisenberg & Sons. Clothing with Irma Kirby labels, either from her own limited line or the Eisenberg & Sons Original designs bearing her name, are rare and should be treasured when found.

When Kirchner returned to Eisenberg & Sons, it was with other designers now on staff. They had been brought in to handle her absence and to oversee the new areas of fashion the company had entered. Irma was returning to do what she did best, design singular creations.

We haven't seen any mention of her retiring, and it is possible that she was still there when the clothing was discontinued in 1958, as she would only have been in her sixties. There is also no date of death listed for her that we could find.

AGNINI & SINGER. Agnini & Singer was founded in Chicago in 1921 as the Oreste Agnini Company. Agnini was an Italian immigrant who came to America in 1903 and used his drawing skills as a war observer behind enemy lines in WWI. He turned his artistic hand to jewelry design after the war when he founded the first jewelry manufacturing business in Chicago.

Shortly after getting the company up and running, he brought in Ralph Singer as a full partner, changing the company name to Agnini & Singer. Singer was also an Italian immigrant and had worked in the jewelry industry as a stone setter in New York before joining Agnini in Chicago.

Agnini & Singer contracted with many companies to manufacture buttons, buckles, and jewelry, but their most famous client was Eisenberg & Sons. They used only the finest stones, the most sophisticated settings, unequaled mold techniques, and showcased a truly magnificent hand of design. Sadly, none of these early pieces were marked, making it difficult to establish Agnini & Singer as Eisenberg's designers. Many of the early fixings and jewelry pieces acknowledged for their quality and design are likely theirs. The newly discovered design card archive offers hope of identifying some of these pieces.

Agnini & Singer launched their own line of jewelry in the 1940s, called ORA. The ORA pieces marked from the 1940s are lovely and quite difficult to come by. Later pieces, from the 1950s on, appear on the market fairly regularly, often bearing the marks ORA Creations and ORA Originals.

In 1952, Agnini retired, selling his half of the business to Singer, who created the Ralph Singer Company. It is still operating today, though there are no more Singers in the company, as it was sold to the Smith family in 1984. One of Singer's daughters said that when her father purchased the company, it was with the belief that one of his three daughters would eventually take over. She worked on the production floor growing up and has fond memories of watching the magnificent pieces being made.

However, life would shift the focus of the daughters away from the business, and when Singer died in 1963, son-in-law Raymond Pausback took on the management with Ralph's widow, Celeste, and eventually bought her out. When he sold the business in 1984, it was still successfully using the original molding processes that had made the company famous, and only the finest of materials were utilized. Today Stanford Smith II and his wife Carole, run the Ralph Singer Company. They are immensely respected in the industry for their quality creations, particularly their fraternal order pieces.

REINAD NOVELTY CO. The Reinad company began in 1922 as Chanel Novelty Co. For years it existed solely as a designer and manufacturer of fixings and jewelry pieces that were marketed under other labels. In 1941 Reinad showed the first pieces the company was marketing under its own label. Naturally, these pieces went out with the mark "Chanel" in script, and the company was immediately attacked by Maison Chanel of Paris—Coco Chanel. The company quickly changed its name to Reinad Novelty Co. It continued to make pieces for other labels, and in limited numbers for its own house, until the mid-1950s, when the company closed.

There is some debate over the large number of duplications of designs credited to Reinad. In June 2015, an article in *Costume Jewelry Collectors International* argues that Reinad may not have actually worked for these high-end companies, but rather may have been copying designs done by other manufacturers.[1]

Reinad may have simply been marketing the same design to multiple clients, either at the same time or by recycling earlier creations. It may also have been creating the same pieces to be marketed at different consumer levels. There is very little information about its designs, or the company itself. So while Reinad did make some amazing pieces, we simply do not know the true story, or the facts of its involvement with Eisenberg.

FALLON & KAPPEL AND EISENBERG, PART 1. Fallon & Kappel was founded in New York in 1928, on the upper floor of the Eaves Costume Building at 151 West 46th Street. Using only the most magnificent imported stones, incredible molding techniques, and detailed finishing work, they established themselves at the top level of costume jewelry manufacturing. In the 1930s, when they took on Eisenberg as a client, they already had prestigious label clients like Chanel, Hattie Carnegie, and Schiaparelli.

Eisenberg entered into jewelry at the same high level of quality that they strove for in their clothing, and working with a premier house like F&K was a major investment. Jewelry with the Eisenberg Original mark could cost the equivalent of a woman's monthly salary.

In 1940 F&K hired a young Ruth Kamke, and though other designers would come and go over the years, Kamke was the only one who stayed until the company closed. Kappel and Kamke kept a close eye on the market so they could figure out which designs to focus on and which pieces should be marketed to which buyers. In an interview with Nicholas and Linda Tollemache, "Vintage Fashion and Costume Jewelry" (date unknown), Kamke stated that she mostly just designed what she was inspired to create, and if there was a guiding hand, it was certainly never trying to tell her what to design.

Fallon & Kappel were not opposed to inspiration. If it could be made—and Kamke had learned exactly what could go from sketch to mold to finished product—they would consider offering it to clients. For Eisenberg this meant as many as two figurals a collection, but never more than four. Figural pieces never sold as well as abstract designs. In collecting jewelry today, the opposite is true; themed pieces are the most sought after.

There were either two main collections a year, with an additional cruise selection, based on what Kamke said in an interview with Nicholas Tollamache, or there were four collections a year based upon what she stated to author Kathy Flood. Both answers are probably right if we take into account just how many years of production we are talking about. Any time period talking about "cruise-specific" creations is most definitely taking place in the early years of F&K's manufacturing for Eisenberg. The increase in collections would have come later as seasonal marketing would be adopted within the industry.

What makes our heads spin is that even when we count every floral creation we have ever seen as a figural (and yes, that might be pushing it), we struggle to come up with enough figural designs to match the number that were likely made. Yet every time we think, "Can there possibly be that many figurals out there?" we are surprised to discover a new piece.

In 1943, as the war was squeezing the supply of materials, Kappel agreed to an exclusivity contract with Eisenberg. This must have caused quite a ruckus among the other clients, but it was a relationship that would continue profitably for almost thirty years.

This also marked the beginning of the sterling years. Even though the war had also affected the availability of sterling, enough was available from North American mines and from the smelting of existing sterling creations to meet the industry's needs. Kamke commented that she saw some magnificent things melted that she felt were far more important than the jewelry they would become, but Eisenberg collectors treasure the Original sterling creations.[2]

F&K had to get creative when the stockpiles of European crystals and stones ran out and "American Ice" was substituted. Considered inferior for its lack of brilliance, F&K stripped off the foil backings and many times set the pieces into open settings to allow for the most sparkle possible.

Sterling was phased out in 1948 and rhodium took over. However, for a brief period, Eisenberg marketed rhodium over sterling pieces, sterling pieces, and non-sterling rhodium pieces at the same time. Eventually European stones were back on the scene allowing a return to the far more brilliant sparkle of earlier pieces. Yet after the sterling years, F&K's creations for Eisenberg would never quite be the same.

FALLON & KAPPEL AND EISENBERG PART 2. Kappel ran F&K until the late 1940s, as Fallon had passed away a decade earlier. He relied heavily on his manager, Florence Nathan, who brought her husband, Murray Silverman, into the company in 1945, also as a manager. In the late 1940s, the couple purchased the business from Kappel. Nathan appears to have been behind the design side of things, with Silverman's name coming up mostly in relation to the nuts and bolts of the business.

Nathan is often erroneously credited as a designer because many of the patents bear her name as the filer. However, Nathan did have a strong hand in design. She worked closely with Kappel to refine the designs presented to clients. There were twenty-seven designs patented in 1942—a bracelet and twenty-six brooches, one a glorious figural swan with pink stones. Later patents are held by Silverman.

As the sterling years ended, the pressure was on to supply larger quantities for Eisenberg's expanding and less exclusive franchise market. This meant that Nathan and Silverman had to make sure Kamke was providing simpler yet trendy designs. Though market tastes were moving toward smaller and more delicate creations, and cost had become a prime consideration, the new owners were struggling.

In Kamke's lengthy interview with Nicholas Tollamache from 2000, we learn many details about F&K. According to Kamke, when F&K employees tried to unionize in the early 1950s, Nathan and Silverman closed up shop and moved their manufacturing to a union-free Long Island facility. The rest of their business was conducted in Eisenberg's headquarters and showroom space in Manhattan.[3]

Kamke stayed in Manhattan, but the rest of the skilled craftsmen were replaced with far less experienced non-union staff. Consequently, the quality of the Eisenberg jewelry began to decline. Rather than the stones being prong-set, they were now glued in place. Construction was not as intricate as in the past. F&K's Eisenberg pieces continued to be of higher design and fabrication quality than their competition. But it was no longer possible to spot an Eisenberg piece across the room, and it was less likely for Eisenberg to be compared to high-end designers. The line was still selling well and the relationship between the two companies was still strong as the 1950s ended.

In the 1960s, the market would drastically shift. New techniques practiced in Rhode Island made the market far more competitive and drove down prices. Demand for high-end costume jewelry continued to diminish. Fashion magazines were removing costume jewelry from their pages, leaving companies with only purchased advertising to attract consumers. F&K tried to stick to their guns, but the cracks were showing.

Eisenberg started to make unmarked pieces. The designs were far from distinct and seemed to be based far more on production cost and market price than on brand recognition, a decision that would prove tragic.

By the 1970s, the owners seem to have gotten tired of it all. In 1972 they announced that in just two weeks F&K would be no more. It was a shock, especially to their thirty-two-year employee, Ruth Kamke. Unforgivable, and quite baffling, was their decision to literally burn the business to the ground. According to Kamke, all records, molds, and designs were either hauled off to the dump or incinerated.[4] If it weren't for the actual pieces that have been preserved, it would be as if the company had never existed.

RUTH KAMKE. When one thinks of Eisenberg jewelry, one must acknowledge that it had a queen, and her name was Ruth Kamke. What Irma Kirby was for Eisenberg fashion, Kamke was for its jewelry. Kamke didn't join Fallon & Kappel until 1940, so there are designs from F&K for Eisenberg that pre-date her arrival, and freelance designs were used regularly until after the exclusivity contract between F&K and Eisenberg was signed in 1943. Other designers also came and went, but they didn't stay long enough to have an impact. From the moment F&K realized what Kamke was capable of, they allowed her imagination, creativity, and professionalism to guide the company's style.

Kamke hadn't planned on a jewelry career; she focused on fashion as a child, but she needed an income and was just fifteen when she applied to F&K for a job as an enameller. She won the position by bringing in a fashion design sketchbook in which she had created individual jewelry pieces to match her original clothing. Since dresses with adornments were a staple of one of F&K's largest clients, Eisenberg, they snapped her up. A week later they made her their sole in-house designer.

Her first job was to create pieces for the Eaves Costume Company that shared the building. Eaves was the largest stage costume supplier in New York and apparently Kamke designed pieces specifically for them. She pointed only to the enchanting brooch "Piggy Goes To Market" as an Eaves-commissioned piece that ended up being sold by Eisenberg. Are there others? Well, given that "Piggy" is a full-bodied pig wearing a shawl and has an articulated swinging basket dangling from its arm, we can only hope so.

figure 8.1

Kamke was a professional and diligently learned the art of manufacturing from the expert model makers F&K employed. She came to understand the limitations and possibilities of the process, whereas many of the freelance submissions were beautiful but they couldn't be cost-effectively made into molds. Kamke's reputation comes from her ability to create elaborate pieces that could be produced in large numbers. And not until the exclusivity deal was struck with Eisenberg did she know who her client was. Hundreds of her pieces were produced each year. She found inspiration everywhere she went and spent a lot of time studying seasonal colors and the stones she would have to work with.

After F&K abruptly closed its door, Kamke would design both precious and costume jewelry as a freelancer, and though she enjoyed crafting pieces to be made with fine metals, she hated the lack of stability and the isolation of working on her own. Panetta, a company known for its costume versions of fine jewelry, was a major purchaser of her designs. In fact, the owners were two brothers, Armando and Amadeo Panetta, who had worked as stone-setters for Eisenberg years earlier. By 1947, Kamke was working for them full-time. Her designs were very different from what she had done for Eisenberg, yet they are just as amazing.

In Kamke's forty-eight years of designing jewelry, it would be impossible to speculate how many designs she drew and how many pieces were made. Her remarkable legacy is appreciated every day by the collectors and jewelry lovers around the world who own and wear her designs.

figure 8.1 Piggy Goes to Market, c. 1940s. Designed by Ruth Kamke for Eaves Costume Co. Sold by Eisenberg. A full-bodied pig wearing a shawl has an articulated swinging basket dangling from its arm. *From the Collection of Bobye Syverson.*

EISENBERG—AFTER FALLON & KAPPEL. The 1970s were profitable for Eisenberg jewelry, as they continued to fulfill contracts for some very interesting pieces. There would be Asian and Egyptian themed pieces, designs that incorporated Millefiori glass stones and faux agate, and more figural pieces. Of course, their hand-painted enamels with 18K gold electroplating are probably their best-known, and quite collectible, 1970s creations. All pieces during this period were marked Eisenberg or E.

The three-generational legacy ended in 1977 when Karl Eisenberg merged the company into Berns-Friedman, which provided jewelry for mid-level department stores. He is still listed as trademark owner of "Eisenberg Ice" and continued to have a hand in the jewelry line. This was the first time Eisenberg jewelry had the signature "Eisenberg Ice," despite the phrase's association with the company dating back to the 1930s.

Eisenberg Ice jewelry did well in the 1980s and 1990s. This was the period when the Original pieces began to become collectable, spawning a resurgence of interest in the Eisenberg name. Berns-Friedman would capitalize on this, first by making some pieces that bear eerie similarity to Kamke's 1950s and 1960s designs. Then they would take inspiration from even further back by marketing "Classics" pieces that were modern versions of some of the Eisenberg Original designs.

Eisenberg Ice would also become a highly collectable name for the Christmas-themed jewelry they were selling. In fact early Eisenberg Ice Christmas trees are quite desirable among the holiday collectors.

In *Warman's Costume Jewelry Figurals*, Flood notes that Eisenberg was the first costume jewelry company to "feature an African-American model" and the first to "feature a nude model."

Eventually, under competitive pressure, the pieces began to be unmarked once more. They were sold with paper hang tags or on blister cards. Once those were removed, the pieces became anonymous.

The last mention we found of an active line was in 2011, and Berns-Friedman has gone out of business. Sadly, this brought to an end a jewelry line that had lasted for over seventy-five years.

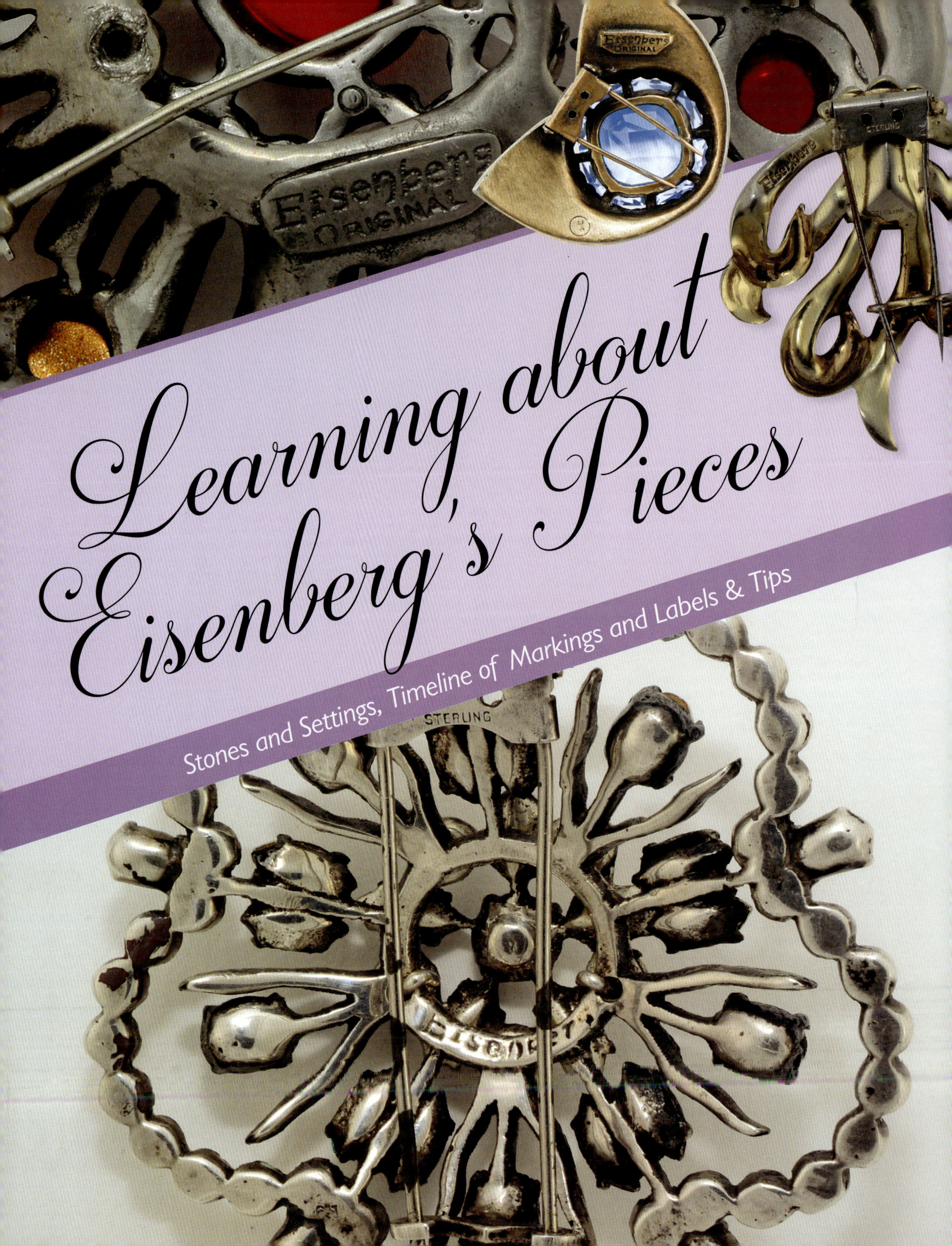

Eisenberg ORIGINAL
Eisenberg ORIGINAL
Learning about Eisenberg's Pieces
Stones and Settings, Timeline of Markings and Labels & Tips
STERLING

Austrian crystals. Originally referred to as diamante or paste, these "imitation" stones were created as replacements for costly gems and originated with Georg Friedrich Strass in the late eighteenth century. They are a composite of leaded glass, rock crystal, and acrylic, and when coated mimic a gem's sparkle. At the time they were quality imposters. Historically, Austrian stones have had a high lead content, which gives them a superior shine.

Bezel set. Bezel-set stones are each encircled with their own metal setting. The stones are sunk within the setting, creating a low profile, but they continue to offer sparkle due to the faceting of the stone.

Brooch. Brooches, or pins, date back to very early times, as they were used to keep garments closed. The word "pin" can be used for description, but in modern understanding the term brooch implies ornamental, which is why we chose to use it.

Cabochon. From the French word caboche or "head," the term applies to stones that are cut and polished, not faceted. Most rhinestones will not be cabochons as faceting is what gives them their sparkle.

Costume jewelry. This term has been used since the 1920s to describe jewelry made with non-precious materials. Originally it could be used as a derogatory term, but is now simply used as a classification. It is now recognized that many manufacturers of costume jewelry designed and crafted their pieces with skill and attention not always present in "fine" jewelry.

Cut and shape of stones. Terms such as marquis, round, emerald, etc., refer to the shape the stone has been cut into. There are some variations and overlapping of names for the styles within the jewelry world.

Demi-parure. This refers to a two-piece matched set of jewelry that is part of a larger set. Some twentieth-century jewelry was manufactured and sold as multiple matching pieces that allowed consumers to select the combinations they wanted. Two matching pieces may have been purchased that way, or a larger set may have lost a mate through the years.

Dress clip. Dress clips are hinged bars that run down the back of the piece. They are worn clamped over a garment edge, but can be clipped to hats and handbags just as easily. They have teeth along the inside of the bar to grip the fabric.

Enamel. Enameling a piece involves adding a layer of color to an existing finish. It actually starts as a powder in the desired shade, which is then heated until it melts into a coating. Enameling shows wear fairly easily but creates striking colors.

Faceted. Faceting is a technique used to create sparkle from stones. Tiny angled cuts are made to the surface area to refract and reflect light. The process goes back to the 1600s.

Foil backed. A stone with an applied "mirror" or metallic finish to its rear to reflect the light back up and through the stone is foil backed. On high quality stones, this really enhances the sparkle.

Fur clip. Fur clips are distinguished by pronged tines with pointed tips and are hinged at the top. They were designed to pierce through fur and anchor the piece.

Gold plated. Plating is a term used for adding a layer of gold to a metal not naturally gold colored. It will always be of noticeable thickness. It is called vermeil when done to sterling. The terms gold filled and gold tone are also used to describe a piece with gold plating.

Gold wash. Gold wash is a very thin layer of gold over another metal. A piece is "dipped" or "burnished" with just a coating of gold. This is much more easily worn away than plating.

Open backed. Occasionally, for style reasons, a rhinestone will not have a foil backing. This also occurs sometimes with lower-quality stones that do not reflect much light, as they are less clear. Removing the backing allows light to also enter from the rear, creating more shine.

Parure. The term comes from the French verb "to adorn" and references sets of jewelry. It dates to the seventeenth century, when a parure could consist of an entire wardrobe of pieces that shared a theme, from hair adornments to shoe buckles and all the bits in between. The word evolved to mean pieces of matching design. Now the term is used for a set of at least three matching pieces.

Paste. Paste is a term referring to glued in stones. Higher-quality manufacturing avoids the use of glue and all larger stones will likely be prong set.

Pavé set. Pavé set stones are grouped closely together, creating a seamless sea of sparkle. They do not have individual settings but are placed within indentations on a single piece of metal.

Pot metal. In the jewelry industry, the term is synonymous with "white metal" or "base metal." It is basically non-precious, low-melting-temperature metals that were easily cast and molded. "Pot metal" seems to have come from the automotive industry that mixed salvaged metal in one pot.

Prong set. Prong-set stones are held in place by metal tines that bend over and "hold" the stone. While we do not list prong set in our descriptions for space purposes, we do point out when pieces have pavé or bezel set stones.

Swarovski rhinestones. The explosion of the modern rhinestone started with Daniel Swarovski in the late 1800s. He augmented the sparkle of Austrian stones by adding a permanent foil backing for additional light reflection. This also allowed him to mimic almost any stone. He patented a mechanical cutting process that allowed for mass production. The term "rhinestone" comes from his location near the Rhine River in Austria.

Vermeil. Vermeil is used to describe gold plating done to sterling, a naturally non-gold-colored material.

Additionally, we used some abbreviations to shorten descriptions: Accents refers to accent stones; clears refers to clear rhinestones; and sets refers to set stones, often preceded by a pavé or bezel quantifier. Measurements are shown as height by width.

Clothing Labels

The earliest Eisenberg & Sons Original clothing label is always cross-stitched and features non-script writing, but with a flourish. The oldest pieces we have seen bearing this label are from the early 1930s, but we suspect 1920s pieces would be similarly labeled.

During this period there was also a rare larger label with additional wording at the bottom that read, "Designed by Irma Kirby." Sadly we were unable to find a sample.

By the end of the 1930s, the label had changed. It still had the basic lettering design, but showed a variation of the figural lady that would become Eisenberg's signature.

The Suwanee Ensembles label appeared in the late 1930s. We have at least two known variations dating to the mid-1940s. We cannot be sure when the primary label changed, but pieces from the mid-1940s are bearing labels with a new design.

While the 1940s would see "Eisenberg Originals" being used in advertising and to mark some items, the label does not seem to begin on the clothing until around 1950. It would be the last re-design and would be used until the end of the clothing line in 1958.

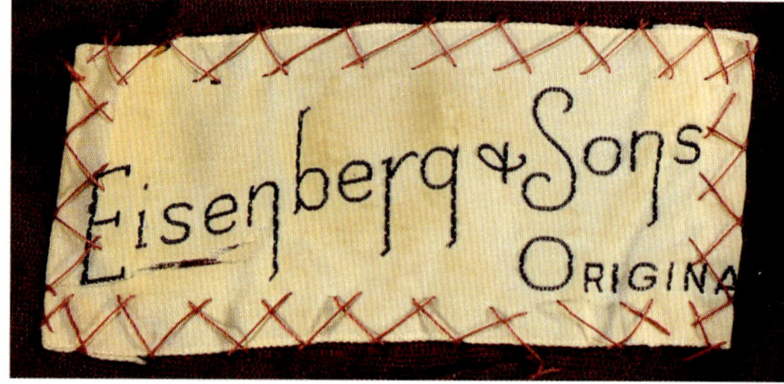

figure 9.1 Early label.

figure 9.2 Early label.

figure 9.3 Early version of the Suwanee Ensembles label. *From the Collection of Joanna van Ritbergen.*

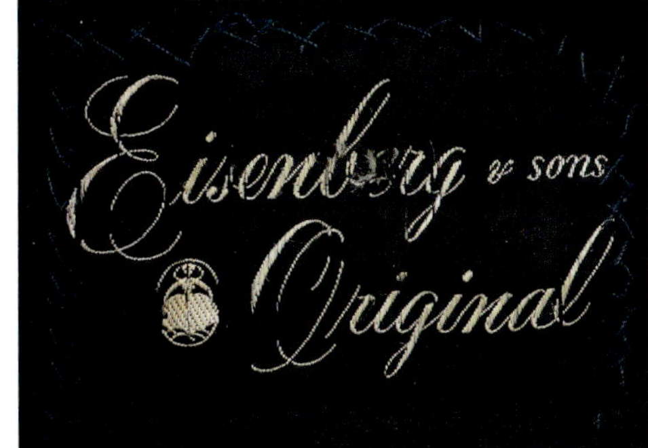

figure 9.4 Early label.

figure 9.5 Early label.

figure 9.6 Later version of the Suwanee Ensembles label. *From the Collection of Laura Sutton.*

figure 9.7 Early label.

Jewelry Markings

The earliest Eisenberg jewelry was marked "Eisenberg Original" and the pieces were made of pot metal. These pieces could be gold washed, gold plated, be given antiqued finishes, coated (which has a more polished patina), or left unfinished, which has a dull appearance similar to pewter.

There were two versions of the signature—a simple handwritten-style Eisenberg Original or a dot matrix Eisenberg with handwritten-style Original.

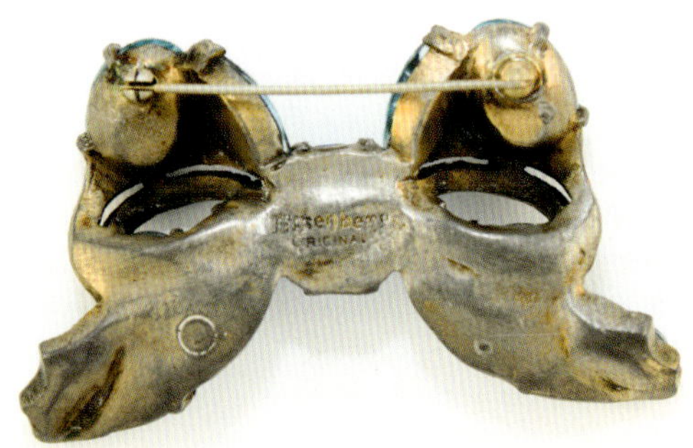

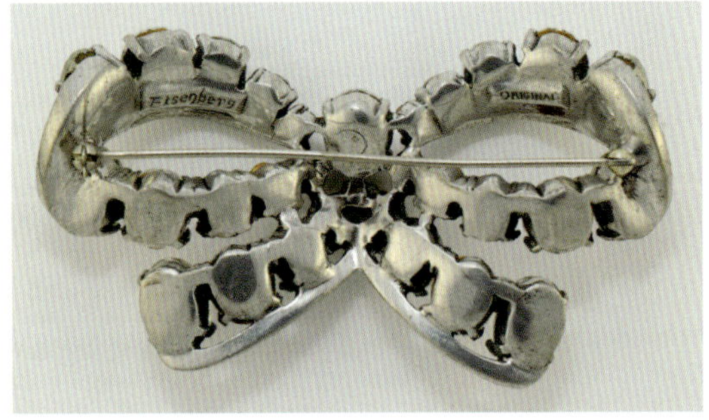

From the mid-1930s to 1943, there were three different types of signature. Pieces could be marked directly on the fabric, marked on an affixed plaque, or, in the cases of dress clips, the mark was often only on the clip back.

There were instances when "Eisenberg" and "Original" would appear on different parts of the pieces, and there were times where there was simply no room for "Original." A few pieces from this period have only a script E.

Both the script and dot matrix versions of the signature continued through the sterling years between 1943 and 1948. But there were only two presentations during these years—on the piece, or on an affixed plaque. "Sterling" was marked on the pieces, either with the Eisenberg Original signature or somewhere else.

A number of Eisenberg Original pieces during this period are only marked "Eisenberg" and "Sterling." There is no clear reason why "Original" was sometimes omitted, except on pieces where space was limited. There are even sterling pieces with the "E." Eisenberg sterling Mexican pieces are always hand-signed in cursive.

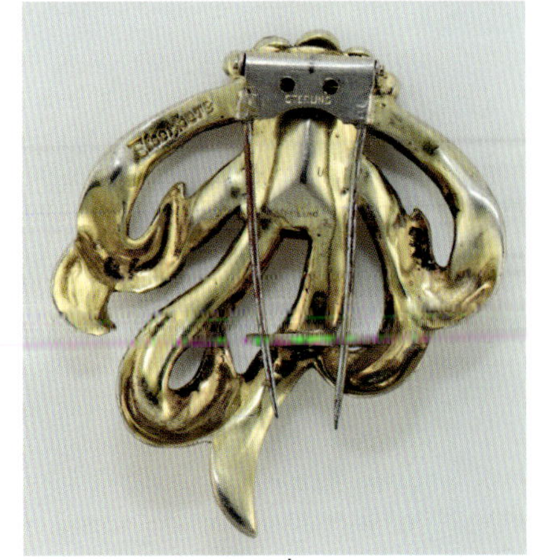

There were four different marks between 1948 and 1958. The earliest designs from this period appear to mainly have the script E and handwritten Eisenberg (the same as during the Original years, only now not on sterling.) It appears that later pieces tended to have the block Eisenberg and the block E. Yet there are block E pieces that are sterling and even a few rhodium pieces that are marked Eisenberg Original. The single script E also appears throughout the entire timeline we cover. Nearly identical pieces can be marked differently, and these four marks could come from any part of this period.

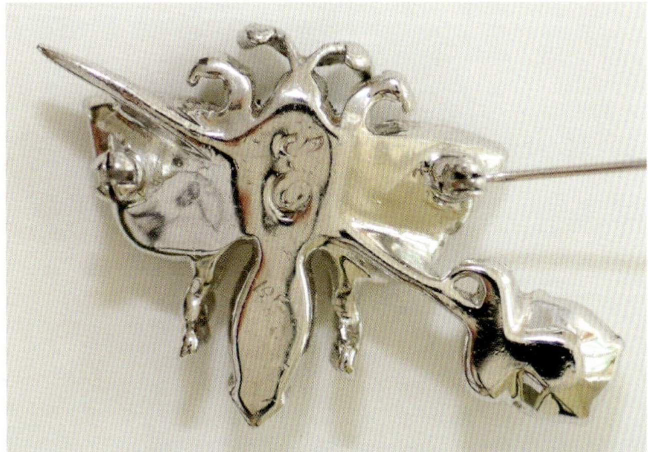

Stone setters also left their mark. These appear as single letters or numbers, sometimes within circles. During our research we found that much is being inferred from the presence of these marks, even when the piece is not marked Eisenberg. Their presence does not indicate an Eisenberg piece. It simply indicates that the piece was made in one of the design houses where setters signed the pieces they worked on. F&K employed this technique, as the marks can be found on their sterling pieces. We even have F&K manufactured rhodium pieces for Eisenberg that bear setters' marks.

Prior to their exclusivity contract with Eisenberg, F&K would have made pieces for other clients that also bore setters' marks. So the presence of a setter's mark is in no way a confirmation of an Eisenberg design. The piece needs to be marked with one of Eisenberg's signatures.

What about unsigned pieces? Reputable dealers, experienced collectors, even "experts" have put Eisenberg's name to unsigned pieces. This is understandable since these pieces were clearly made by the same companies, were crafted using the same techniques and components, and were imagined by the same designers. That does not mean they are Eisenberg pieces. Our research has shown that Eisenberg took marking their pieces very seriously. From the start of the jewelry line until roughly 1958, all pieces sold by Eisenberg were marked, with two possible exceptions.

One is pieces within a parure; it appears that if the set was packaged to be sold together, not every piece was marked. We have included a few such pieces in this book that do not have an Eisenberg signature, and we have stated as much, and explained why we believe it is appropriate to include them.

The second exception would be the very early creations from Agnini & Singer. Here again, there is simply no way to differentiate between pieces they made for Eisenberg & Sons and pieces they made for their other clients. We still have hope that some of these pieces can be claimed someday through the design cards stored at Ralph Singer Company.

Collectors also may find the same pieces both marked and unmarked. We have seen this ourselves. Again, though, Eisenberg marked their pieces. It could be a re-sold design. It might have been a piece purchased by another client as well as Eisenberg. The mark may have worn off or been polished off. It might be a period copy. It might have originally been part of a set. It could even be an Eisenberg that somehow missed being signed. The lack of an Eisenberg signature has to be properly considered, but it does mean that the piece should not be given the provenance of having actually been sold by Eisenberg.

What does that do to value? When we speak of value, we use the standards typically used by insurance companies. If you insure your collection, add a rider to your policy, or claim a loss, the company will want to know about your pieces. If the piece is to be valued as an Eisenberg, they will expect it to be marked.

But unsigned pieces are certainly not without value, because they were crafted by the same hands that gave us the magnificent Eisenberg creations. They are marvelous examples of skill and quality and are quite valuable. They should never be dismissed or undervalued. They just should not be thought of as Eisenberg pieces.

So if you are collecting Eisenberg, look for the proper markings. If you collect vintage jewelry, then eagerly snap up other pieces in good condition if they appeal to you.

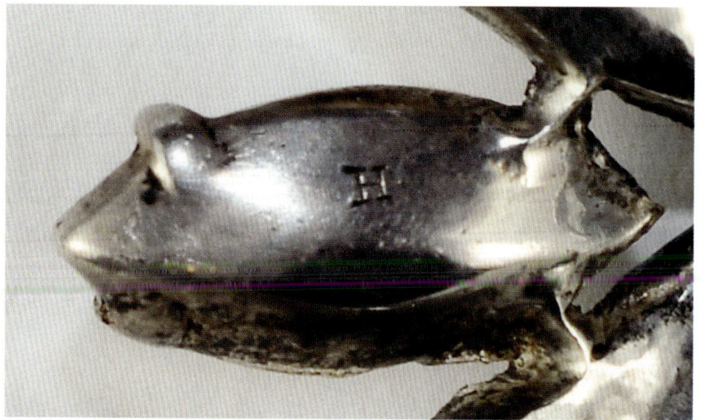

Eisenberg Original Hardware

Some of the earliest dress clips were actually tiny in comparison to some of the designs they were supposed to support. They appear in the 1930s. Throughout the Original years, the dress clip back would stay the same.

In the 1930s and 1940s, the fur clip that adorned Eisenberg clothing always seems to have had two holes on the bar at the hinge. Does this mean that only one company provided fur clips? Possibly. This consistency may also have been an anti-counterfeiting move.

The earliest fur clips were two-pronged with the holes on the bar. Later in the 1940s, Eisenberg began adding hooks as safety catches for the prongs. Eisenberg fur clips were often large and heavy; they were also quite expensive and needed something secure to hold them in place. The 1950s fur clips had a completely different design. Some Eisenberg Original pieces are actually multiple pieces affixed to one another with screws or rings.

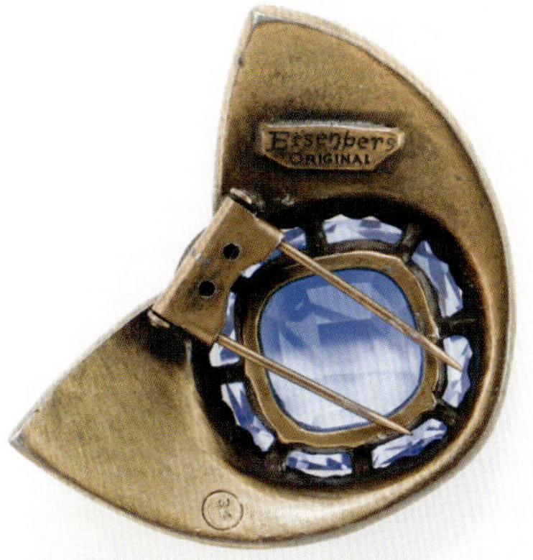

Collecting Tips

How do I know my Eisenberg Original is genuine?

That is a tricky question. During the late 1980s through the 1990s, there was an explosion in counterfeits hitting the market. Some of these counterfeits are very good, even to the quality of their fake markings. Even today, the climbing value of vintage costume jewelry results in counterfeit pieces being made and sold.

Some of the fake Eisenberg Original pieces are of such magnificent quality that collectors have bought them knowing they were reproductions. Collectors call these pieces "reproductions by artists," as they are lovely. These pieces are often on the market from secondary hands that usually do not know they are not genuine. Spotting them can be difficult.

What should you look for? First, look for the mark. Also consider the hardware. The quality of the finishing details can call a piece into question; genuine Eisenberg Original pieces were manufactured by high-end companies and the work should show it.

Affixed plaques should match in metal and should be attached with care and little sign of solder. We have seen quite a few "added" plaques.

Many high-end reproductions were done in copper, and though some Eisenberg Original pieces have unique patinas, none of them were manufactured with copper.

Eisenberg Original pieces should have all their larger stones prong set. This is not the best way to judge a piece, as most people marketing Originals they knew were not genuine used vintage pieces that were prong set.

Many of these "newly marked" Eisenbergs were probably originally unmarked Reinad and F&K pieces, or pieces from houses of equal caliber, so the quality difference is imperceptible. We are sure that over time some of these will end up being considered Eisenbergs, since without detailed records of all the pieces Eisenberg sold, it is often impossible to tell the difference.

What about condition?

As with anything people collect, condition affects value. Eisenberg's jewelry creations have seen many decades and have usually been worn often. A mint condition find is rare, particularly for Eisenberg Original pieces. Yet pieces with significant wear or that have damage should be avoided.

What can be fixed?

Stones. When clear stones begin to gray, only small stones are likely to be available for replacement. When matching stones can be found, proper techniques need to be used for the installation.

If stones are missing, you will likely only be able to find small stones in common cuts, and color will be limited. People have taken from one vintage piece to fix another when the stone is larger, colored, or uniquely cut, and the matching replacement can be unnoticeable. Any unique components such as beads are probably not replaceable.

Eisenberg jewelry was prong-set for most of its life, but the pavé stones were glued in. Over time some of these have yellowed. Fixing this would require removing the stone, professionally cleaning all residue (although this could remove any wash or plating), and then refitting the stone. However, if the stone is foil-backed, once you remove the stone it is unlikely you will be able to use it again as most of the foil will have stayed with the glue.

Stones develop "flecks" or black spots when the foil on the back of the pieces separates from the stone. It can happen to large or small stones. This can be fixed only by replacing the stone with a matching foil-backed one. The availability of a replacement will depend on the stone but is unlikely for anything but the smallest and simplest of stones.

If a stone is chipped, all you can do is replace it with a matching one. This is unlikely with a stone that is large, colored, or intricately cut. Some people think minor chips are not a big problem, but it should be considered when figuring out what to pay, or conversely, what to charge.

It is much easier to find replacement stones for pieces from the late 1940s, and there are even "new old stock" stones available.

Hardware. It happens. Things break. Qualified estate jewelers can affix a replacement if they have a similar vintage piece and a delicate touch. Unfortunately, we have seen many globs of solder attaching new hardware, and that affects value. If you really want to properly restore a piece and your local jeweler doesn't have what you need, you can watch for pieces of the same metal and design that are beyond repair. These can be purchased relatively inexpensively, and then you can salvage the hardware. There is also a tendency for people to turn fur clips into brooches. It is understandable, as faux fur is not often worn these days. However, the fur clip and dress clip back designs that grace Eisenberg's pieces may not be so easily found.

Finish. Most Eisenberg Original pieces will have scratched, nicked, or worn finishes where the base color shines through. If the wear is minimal it is unlikely to affect value or your ability to resell the piece. The more wear there is, the more difficult it will be to sell, and that drives the price down. Usually it comes down to your own preferences and intentions.

You can "re-dip" a rhodium piece, but the cost is prohibitive as everything would have to be removed, and the jeweler will charge you for labor as well as the new plating.

Enamel. Enameling is one of the aspects most prone to show wear. It should never be touched up. We have never seen a "fixed" enameling job on an Eisenberg piece that has been acceptable. There are expert restorers who can do the work, but the cost is not justifiable.

Basically, you should always buy for your own desires. If you love the piece and want to wear it, then the condition is obviously acceptable. Pay what you are comfortable paying, with the understanding of how others might judge the piece.

If you are buying for a collection, keep in mind how easy or difficult it will be to sell down the line. Many distinctive Eisenberg Original pieces are quite expensive; make sure the condition is equal to the price.

Chapter 2. A Design Evolution

1. Lisa Hix, "Rhinestone Dynasty: Karl Eisenberg Talks About His Family's Costume Jewelry,"

2. Robin Deutsch, "Who Was Reinad? Creator or Copier?"

3. Nicholas Tollamache, "The Designs of Ruth Kamke."

Chapter 3. The Sweet Smell of Success

1. Jacquelyne North, *Perfume, Cologne, and Scent Bottles*, p. 131.

Chapter 5. Did You Know They Made Those?

1. Alice Hughes, "Hang Your Painting on the Wall as a Mural or Wear It on Your Shoulders Like a Scarf."

2. Maribeth Keane and Ben Marks, "To Restore or Not to Restore? A Look at Vintage Rhinestone Jewelry."

3. Bobye Syverson, "show and tell 2", http://imageevent.com/bobye/showandtell2.

Chapter 7. In Style

1. Women's Wear Daily, June 4, 1941, p 21.

Chapter 8. The Stories Behind the Names

1. Robin Deutsch, "Who Was Reinad? Creator or Copier?"

2. Nicholas Tollamache, "The Designs of Ruth Kamke."

3. Ibid.

Bibliography

Ancestry.com. "Deaths and Stillbirths 1916–1947." http://www.ancestry.com-Illinois.

Bagdade, Susan Klein. "Eisenberg & Ralph Singer Jewelry: A Tale of Two Companies." Costume Jewelry Collectors International, Nov. 2, 2014, http://www.costumejewelrycollectors.com/2014/11/02/eisenberg-ralph-singer-jewelry-tale-two-companies.

Becker, Vivenne, Nicoletta Bocca, Gerda Buxbaum, Deanna Farneti Cera, Melissa Garbardi, Vera Maternova, Eduard Schwaiger, Alfred M. Weisberg. *Jewels of Fantasy, Costume Jewelry of the 20th Century.* New York, NY: Harry N. Abrams, Inc., 1991.

Brunialti, Carla Ginelli, Roberto Brunialti. *American Costume Jewelry Art & Industry, 1935-1950, A-M.* Atglen, PA: Schiffer Publishing Ltd., 2008.

Brunialti, Carla Ginelli, Roberto Brunialti. *American Costume Jewelry Art & Industry, 1935-1950, N-Z.* Atglen, PA: Schiffer Publishing Ltd., 2008.

Chicago History Museum. "Eisenberg Shop in Chicago (Ill.), 1941." http://chicagohistory.org.

Deutsch, Robin. "Who Was Reinad? Creator or Copier?" Costume Jewelry Collectors International. June 16, 2015, http://www.costumejewelrycollectors.com/2015/06/16/who-was-reinad-creator-or-copier-by-robin-deutsch-for-cjci.

Flood, Kathy. *Warman's Costume Jewelry Figurals—Identification and Price Guide.* Iola, WI: Krause Publications, 2007.

Hix, Lisa. "Rhinestone Dynasty: Karl Eisenberg Talks About His Family's Costume Jewelry." Collectors Weekly, Nov. 26, 2010, http://www.collectorsweekly.com/articles/rhinestone-dynasty-karl-eisenberg-talks-about-his-familys-costume-jewelry.

Hughes, Alice. "Hang Your Painting on the Wall as a Mural or Wear It on Your Shoulders Like a Scarf," Today's Woman, *New York Post,* March 12, 1941.

Keane, Maribeth, Ben Marks. "To Restore or Not to Restore? A Look at Vintage Rhinestone Jewelry." *Collectors Weekly,* February 10, 2010, http://www.collectorsweekly.com/articles/an-interview-with-rhinestone-costume-jewelry-appraiser-and-repairperson-rosalie-sayyah.

Milbank, Caroline Rennolds. *New York Fashion: The Evolution of American Style.* New York, NY: Adams Books, 1996.

Morning Glory Antiques. "Jewel Chat." http://www.morninggloryantiques.com.

North, Jacquelyne. *Perfume, Cologne, and Scent Bottles.* West Chester, PA: Schiffer Publishing, 1986.

Ralph Singer Jewelry. "About Us." http://www.ralphsingerjewelry.com./aboutRalphSingerJewelry.html.

Romero, Christie. *Warman's Jewelry Identification & Price Guide, 3rd Edition.* Iola, WI: Krause Publications, 2002.

Romero, Christie. *Warman's Jewelry Identification & Price Guide, 5th Edition.* Iola, WI: Krause Publications, 2013.

Tollamache, Nicholas. "The Designs of Ruth Kamke." *Vintage Fashion & Costume Jewelry,* Volume 10, No. 1 Winter 2000. http://vfcjblog.wordpress.com.

Wiggins, Pamela Y. *Warman's Jewelry Identification & Price Guide.* Iola, WI: Krause Publications, 2014.

Eisenberg Originals